Libraryland

Libraryland

It's All about the Story

BEN BIZZLE and **SUE CONSIDINE**

ALA
Editions
CHICAGO | 2020

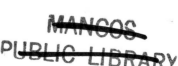
MANCOS
PUBLIC LIBRARY

Extensive effort has gone into ensuring the reliability of the information in this book; however, the publisher makes no warranty, express or implied, with respect to the material contained herein.

ISBNs
978-0-8389-4743-2 (paper)
978-0-8389-4813-2 (PDF)

Library of Congress Cataloging-in-Publication Data
Names: Bizzle, Ben, editor. | Considine, Sue, editor.
Title: Libraryland : it's all about the story / edited by Ben Bizzle and Sue Considine.
Description: Chicago : ALA Editions, 2020. | Summary: "This collection of inspiring first-hand stories from across libraryland spotlights the countless ways in which library staff are making a difference for their communities"—Provided by publisher.
Identifiers: LCCN 2020009881 | ISBN 9780838947432 (paperback) | ISBN 9780838948132 (pdf)
Subjects: LCSH: Libraries and community—United States—Anecdotes. | Librarians—United States—Anecdotes.
Classification: LCC Z716.4 .L53 2020 | DDC 021.2—dc23
LC record available at https://lccn.loc.gov/2020009881

Book design by Alejandra Diaz in the Chaparral Pro and Korolev Rounded typefaces.

♾ This paper meets the requirements of ANSI/NISO Z39.48-1992 (Permanence of Paper).

Printed in the United States of America
24 23 22 21 20   5 4 3 2 1

In Loving Memory

NICOLETTE WARISSE SOSULSKI

She was the best of us.

CONTENTS

INTRODUCTION

t was late one night at a library conference. As is common in library conference culture, friends were sitting around a table in a hotel bar having drinks. I've always been fond of the conference nightlife. It is, to me, where the magic happens. On this particular night, it went something like this . . .

Sue: So Ben, *Start a Revolution: Stop Acting Like a Library* has been out for a few years now. When are you going to write your second book?

Me: I'm not ever writing another book. That was one of the hardest things I've ever done. I left a piece of my soul on those pages.

Sue: Okay, okay, so hypothetically, if you were to write a second book, what would it be?

Me: Well, I'm never going to write another one, but I do have an idea of what I'd do if I was going to . . . which I'm not. I think we need sort of a *Chicken Soup for the Librarian Soul*. There are plenty of instructional books out there, but there's not a lot that's motivational or inspiring. It'd be cool if there was a collection of heart-warming library stories people could reach for when they're having a tough day.

Sue: Oh, that's a great idea. You've got to do it. It would be wonderful.

Me (*this is where my mouth always gets me in trouble*)**:** I'll tell ya what. If you'll do it with me, I'll do it.

Sue (*deliberating for a long moment . . . my heart sinking as I realize she's actually considering this*)**:** Okay, let's do it.

And that was that, no takebacks. That's how this book came into being. A couple of friends at a conference, just planning to have a few drinks, managed to talk themselves into writing a book. Like I said . . . where the magic happens . . .

We know the kinds of challenges you face when working in a library, how tough it can be sometimes. So this book of stories is for you, the compassionate, empathetic, giving people on the front lines of service in your communities. This book is a sharing of the hearts, minds, and spirits of your friends, peers, and colleagues. It is a collection of little notes to inspire you, to soothe you, to lift you up, especially when the everyday gets hard, and to remind you that the work you do is essential. You change and save lives every day.

*Artwork by **Lori Block***

Do You Have Anything on Submarines?

~ NICOLETTE WARISSE SOSULSKI ~

S ometimes, what seems to be the most mundane of reference transactions ends up being the most meaningful of human experiences. That sounds a little Hallmark—okay, a *lot* Hallmark—but several years ago I encountered this in practice.

I was working the desk, and the library, for a change, was relatively quiet. I heard a couple of voices, one growing increasingly frustrated in pitch, over by one of the catalog stations. My curiosity was piqued when I heard the word "submarine," so I went to investigate. I anticipated finding a mother and child struggling with a report of some sort. To the contrary, I found a distinguished couple who seemed to be battling the OPAC with little success.

I caught the woman's eye and she said, "He is trying to find something about submarines, and we can't find anything. Could you help him please?" There was a bit of a tremor in her voice that I did not expect, as my original suspicion of a mother, a child, and a report due tomorrow did not match the somewhat dapper older gentleman with wavy, silvery hair, carefully pressed casual clothes, and an expensive leather jacket.

I approached him and asked, "Are you looking for the history of submarines, how they work, or some story with submarines in the plot?" I was a bit concerned, as I feared the gentleman was perhaps a Tom Clancy reader, and our copy of *The Hunt for Red October* had been literally read to shreds. I was sure it was back on the list of books slated for repair or replacement. I didn't think he was likely to be looking for Jules Verne. The gentleman smiled at me gently and said, "No stories."

I stepped up to the catalog station and, as I suspected, it was set to Subject, the most frustrating field in the library, where extraneous words can virtually ensure that a patron will not find what they're looking for. I could tell that the couple was well-educated, and that the woman especially was not used to a lack of success in a library environment. She had the air of a teacher or somebody who sought out the more challenging book groups, and one who would have opinions on most of the books in the classics canon of forty or so years ago. The gentleman, my immediate patron, continued to smile benignly.

"I can start off by looking for books about submarines and confining my search to the General field. I think we may have a limited book collection on the mechanics of submarines, but I can look for more through our inter-library loan program. Are you interested in their uses in oceanography or historically in warfare?"

"Not oceanography," the gentleman replied, still smiling warmly.

"Well, in history we can also use the term 'U-boat,'" I let him know.

His face lit up and he said, "Yes, yes!"

We walked over to the 600s section, where we found a coffee table book or two, as well as a pictorial history of the development of underwater craft. I gave these books to him somewhat apologetically, saying that we didn't have much with a lot of text or narrative.

I asked, "Do you want to look at these at the table while I go look in the military strategy and history areas?" He nodded and went to the table. To my bemusement, the woman, who by now I had determined was his wife, decided to accompany me instead.

I apologized again for not having more books with more narrative, and she rather sharply responded, "He doesn't read much. The pictures are fine." I must have looked surprised because I would have pegged both of them, from their appearance, as heavy readers.

She continued. "He has Alzheimer's. Right now all he wants to talk about is submarines."

Immediately, and sadly, it made more sense: her tension, his not taking the lead on searching for his own book. I said to her, "I am so sorry."

At that, she crumbled. "He's not the same person he used to be. I can't keep up with him. I have to make sure that he doesn't go wandering off or get lost, so I can't really sleep. I'm so very tired. He's fine now, but he gets so mad at me sometimes."

I could hear the tears in the back of her throat. I touched her shoulder again and repeated how sorry I was. I told her I could not imagine how hard this must be for her, given the changes in the person she was married to and how tired she must be.

Meanwhile, I had found some titles on the use of U-boats in World War II and showed them to her. Many of them had too much text for him to manage, but a few had some great photos. I also found a book/CD combo of historic broadcasts. She said she thought they might be too hard, but I suggested that we put them on the table for him so that he could decide what he did and did not want. Meanwhile, she could search for books for herself and give him some time to look through the things we'd found. She started thanking me profusely, to an extent that far exceeded what I felt I had actually accomplished for them.

We walked over to his table, and I set the books down. I smiled at him and said, "I would like you to see which of these you think will be useful to you and tell me why you like them. Then I can see about getting some more from other libraries for you. I will be back in a minute, but I'm going to also look for some books for your wife."

As we stepped away, she started again. "We used to talk for hours. We used to do things together after work. I'm still trying to work, but I worry about him constantly. We can't talk like that anymore. He either looks at me with that . . . *smile*" [the benign one I had seen earlier, which now seemed far less involved and far more removed]. She practically spat the word *smile*, ". . . or he loses his temper with me. He was never mean to me before."

I touched her shoulder again. "I'm sure I'm not telling you anything that you haven't already considered, but I bet he senses there are things that he can't do or say that he was able to before. It is in no way your fault, but you are the only, or at least the safest, person for him to express his frustrations to. I know that must be really hard for you, but you are the only one there." She nodded and started to tear up and said she was going to get a couple of books while he was occupied. I asked her if she needed any recommendations, but she shook her head and turned away.

I glanced over and he was still happily looking through the books I'd found for him, and I sensed that his wife needed some time to regroup. I checked the desk—no one was there in need of help—and then started doing some searches. I made some printouts, walked over and picked up a book, and sought her out again.

"Ma'am, you have been pretty open with me, so please forgive me if I'm being intrusive, but you sound like you might be at the end of your rope. Your spoons are all used up." I could tell she was not familiar with that phrase, which is popularly used by another exhausted group, those with autoimmune disorders. I clarified: "You start out the day with say 5–7 spoons that have to get you through the day. Performing a task takes up a spoon, a reserve. Maybe time at work uses 3 spoons or getting him ready for something takes 2. When the spoons are gone, so are your mental, emotional, or physical reserves. It sounds like you might be using your spoons up before noon some days, and you never go to bed at night with spares. In the long run that will tear you up."

"Do you fly, ma'am? Or have?" I asked. She nodded. "You know how the flight attendants always caution you to put on your own oxygen mask before helping somebody else?" She nodded again. "Well, you're not doing that, ma'am, and it's taking its toll. I can tell you're a strong person, but everybody has their limits. I'm actually almost more worried about you than I am about him, so I got some things for you." I brought up the printouts. "Have you ever talked to the Alzheimer's Association or the Area Agency on Aging?" She shook her head. "Being a caregiver is one of the hardest jobs in the world. It will never be easy, but they can help you with strategies for getting assistance and, possibly, affordable respite care so that you can go to lunch with a friend or go for a walk. You need to be able to take a break. You have to understand, this is harder than being a mom. Moms don't have the sad memory of a person who doesn't seem to be there anymore. I've printed the contact info for both places. You can also set up an appointment. You need help and you need resources, and the people at both of these places have connections all over the county. You might also be able to find somebody free or affordable to talk to professionally. You're carrying an enormous load, even bigger than you might realize. I have worked with these people, and they can help. And if they can't, please come back and I'll hunt somebody else down for you."

She teared up again and told me that I might have saved her life. "Do you know that nobody else has said anything like this?"

Touched, I replied, "Well, ma'am, it's clear that you are a really strong, capable woman, but you may be doing too good a job [she laughed], and people might think you would be insulted if they offered to help. I'm the kind of person who will say anything if I think it will help someone. I also see these sorts of challenges, in a different way, with lots of people in the library because we're next door to the Senior Center. You need to ask for help. It's okay."

Pulling out the book, I said, "I also have this for you," and I handed her *The 36-Hour Day: A Family Guide to Caring for People Who Have Alzheimer Disease, Other Dementias, and Memory Loss.* "It's not just you. This is a book from Johns Hopkins for people in your situation. People find it helpful. You might too, if only a chapter or paragraph. It's a very popular book and is already in a sixth edition." She had not heard of it and took it gratefully.

"I'm worried about you, ma'am. I can see you've been doing a terrific job, but it's taking its toll on you, and even you are a finite resource. Please try these resources and see if they help, and if they don't, I promise to do everything I can to find something that will," I said.

She hugged me and said I was an angel and that just running into somebody who could offer her anything gave her hope. She said I would never know the difference I had just made. At this point, her husband was approaching with his book selection. He'd settled on three books that he was happy with.

We talked for a few minutes about my finding old newsreels in the future (he had served in World War II). She hugged me again and they headed toward checkout. As I walked away, I heard her telling my coworker that she worked with an angel.

Since then, every time she has come in when I have been on desk—and this has been years—she has hugged me and thanked me again. It is obvious that to her, having a librarian at the right time in her life made her feel as though she was not alone in this bitter battle. Every time I see her, I'm reminded of my power to help and my profession's ability to make a difference. I'm a librarian. We can be lifelines.

Making the Difference

~ FAYETTEVILLE FREE LIBRARY TEAM ~

t's the late 2000s, a truly transformative time for libraries. Libraries are radically redefining their place in the learning ecosystem. Handheld mobile technologies are starting to proliferate in all aspects of our daily life. Social media are exploding, creating new ways for people to connect, debate, think together, share, and create new knowledge. DIY culture is on the rise, and disruptive technologies like 3D printers are beginning to make an entrance into the general public's awareness.

At the Fayetteville Free Library (FFL) in upstate New York, we are responding to the rapid pace of change and the ever-evolving needs, interests, and aspirations of our community. We are busy piloting new products and forging mutually beneficial relationships with industry and community partners to make the patron experience better, more efficient, more contemporary, more interactive, and more satisfying to a broader base.

One day, a talented student support staff member, Lauren, approached our director, Sue, with a new, bold, and radical idea. In a nutshell, Lauren believed that the public library was the perfect platform to provide access to 3D printers, technology that would encourage community members to tinker, create, and learn in new experiential ways in our library. Well, we thought, as we typically did, let's try it! Why not? The suggestion of 3D printers in the library got us to thinking about the wide range of other hands-on opportunities we could provide to the community. We understood that taking the library and the community in this new direction would only be possible by taking small, evenly paced steps. We engaged in the right conversations to provide the staff, board, and key stakeholders with the information and assurances they needed to understand that this would be a journey we would take together, slowly and systematically, learning from success and failure along the way. We experienced many stops and starts, making many right, and just as many wrong, decisions on this new path, but all along we were certain that we were heading in the right direction.

We held open houses where members of the community could come, see, and experience low and high tech, from hand juicers to 3D printers. The excitement from the community was immediately evident; these open houses were drawing large crowds and, even more compellingly, demographics that are notoriously hard to reach, like men in their 30s and 40s and a diverse array of teenagers. People began to approach members of our team saying things like "This is important." "How can I become involved?" "What other kinds of tech will be included?" and more. We were overwhelmed by the response and knew that we were hitting the mark. The community's aspirations and goals and its entrepreneurial potential could, in fact, be well supported by the inclusion and integration of spaces, tools, technology, equipment, and experiences that support creation, invention, and discovery. Suddenly, those who may have never visited our library were beginning to explore and understand the opportunities that could be facilitated there—opportunities that they could get excited about, that they could find personal meaning and value in.

With the assistance of a creative architect, a New York State construction grant award, and the full support of an energized team, we began the process of designing the space and crafting the branding and marketing that would allow us to carry out our vision of "Making" in a public library. We didn't assume that we knew what kind of tech we would include in the spaces. We systematically created opportunities throughout the library spaces for the community to take the lead and tell us what they wanted access to in order to pursue their goals and interests. Our new Making spaces became known as the FabLab.

As more and more people became engaged in our community journey to Making, it became evident that in order to meet all of their needs, we needed to think differently about how we facilitate learning and discovery. Based on the work of John McKnight and Peter Block in the Abundant Community, we embraced the idea that "every community already has what it needs within the community." This was indeed a call to action for us, encouraging us to develop a strategy to reach out into the community to find the people with the talent, expertise, passion, time, and interest to share what they know with their neighbors. One staff cannot possibly possess all the knowledge and expertise that a community needs. Happily, it is not necessary for the staff to overextend or even to learn new things. However, it is essential for the staff to do what we have always done, but to do it more strategically and completely by being active community connectors and facilitators, by creating the conditions that allow neighbors to share what they know with their neighbors.

This approach to engagement was a game changer for the FFL. Suddenly, we were able to provide more sessions on more topics than we could ever have imagined, and in an affordable, community-led way. People came to think very differently about their library and its potential impact on the community.

From our perspective, one of the most powerful results of this journey into Making was the positive impact that Making had on the social structure of the library community. Teens who would not normally cross paths could be seen coding, gaming, and building robots together. Moms in their 30s and 40s were filling in the registration form for Home Repair workshops. Families began spending time making together in one of the three maker-designated spaces in the library. Mutually beneficial, powerful partnerships with non-industry partners allowed us to integrate technologies and software into our labs that would have been cost-prohibitive for us alone. And our library colleagues and peers from around the world began to connect with us, leading to explosive sharing and learning, new ideas and new approaches.

So many truly inspirational moments have happened in the FFL community as a result of Making. In 2013, we were approached by several individuals in our community who were interested in either learning to sew or teaching others how to sew. We immediately put out a call to our community and asked the questions: "Do you sew?" "Would you like to sew with others?" "Would you like to teach others how to sew and share your passion?" We were overwhelmed by the community response. Not only did we receive a tremendous response to our questions, but we also received an overwhelming amount of donations to support sewing in the community, including fabric and buttons, thread, and more. We assessed our budget and realigned our priorities to meet this need and purchased sewing machines that we integrated into our FabLab. Soon the FabLab sewing area was buzzing—seniors teaching teens how to sew, open clubs popping up, the coming together to sew for fun and for purposes like using donated fabric to sew backpack sleeping bags for the homeless population in Syracuse, using pillowcases to make dresses for school-age girls, using fabric to make dog beds for the local animal shelter, and using fabric to make tab blankets for toddlers in the local women's shelter.

All of this activity was gratifying, and clearly these outcomes justified our decision-making. However, a memorable, powerful moment for us was when an elderly woman contacted us to tell her story. She had retired decades earlier and had been sewing alone in her kitchen for years. She had never visited the library, stating, "There was no reason to because there's nothing there for me." A neighbor brought her the flyer we had generated and distributed to gauge the community interest in sewing. The woman decided that she would take the risk and come and see what this was all about. The result: this woman discovered a community, within the larger community, that was just for her. Suddenly, she was no longer sewing alone in her kitchen but sewing with new friends and also teaching others how to sew, including residents from the local agencies and homes for adults with developmental disabilities. She found her passion at the library. She also found herself going out to lunch, the movies, and events in the park with newfound friends. By creating access to sewing machines in the local library, this woman's life was changed, and indeed, transformed.

Many real-world problems have been solved through invention in the FFL FabLab, further proving to us that Making is not a niche endeavor, but a critical element in creating the conditions that allow all kinds of people to develop all kinds of solutions to challenges both big and small. From a pro-grammable toothbrush that helps kids to brush their teeth more effectively, to the development of a brain stem model for use in teaching neuroscience students, to the father who invented an adaptive device to allow his daughter with mobility issues to play and control the music she loves; none of this would have been possible if not for the library.

Undertaking this new direction was a roller-coaster ride. Overall, it was exciting, gratifying, and magical. However, as with all risks and trailblazing, we also hit some of our lowest lows and dealt with some of our most complex failures on this wild and rewarding journey. The journey required a leap of faith for the entire organization, and every member of the team. We had to be patient and professionally generous with each other, understanding that people process and tolerate change in different ways and at different speeds. It was essential to prioritize time for the entire team not only to think and plan together, but also to build the trust capital that would be essential as we moved through the difficult times that this innovation inevitably led us through. It was essential, absolutely critical, for this journey to be a shared one, not one restricted to only a few leaders on the team. The result of this journey on the FFL? A strong, resilient, generous team of professionals and support staff—some of whom remain and some of whom have moved on—who work from their hearts, with a deep respect and understanding of each other, who value the collaborative process, and who know that any journey is better and more successful when we take it together. Nothing will ever keep this stellar team from innovating and staying true to their mission of making their community and the world better.

"Library, huh? It must be great to sit and read all day."

This is the typical reaction I get when I tell people what I do for a living.

I don't get angry. In fact, I smile. Is there an easy way to let people know the path I've taken to get here? Is there any way to let them know that I *chose* this path? Perhaps not.

"Are you a volunteer? You **get paid** to do this?"

What I can do is tell them, and you, my story.

A Golden State (Library) Story

~ CHRISTOPHER GALLEGOS ~

C olorado winters are bitterly cold. New Mexico summers are bru-
tally hot. It was this duo of climate extremes that marked my early
childhood. Aside from seasonal adjustments, the Southwest was a
fantastic place to grow up. Summers were magical. The culture was
as rich as the food, and spinner fishing on the river was one of my favorite
things to do.

By the time I was around ten years old, my folks had completed their college
degrees (Dad was fresh out of an MBA program). We were a tight unit, but
love couldn't remedy the lack of jobs in the Southwest in the early 1990s. My
mom's parents had moved to California in 1988, and they continually asked
us to follow suit and "try it out."

So we went in the summer of 1992. My grandparents hadn't lived in California long enough to have firm roots there, but at least we had someone to
ease us in. We lived in their small apartment for about six months until we
could get our own. It was a new world, but . . . how different could it *really* be?

I found out my first week of school. A series of questions from my school-
mates were pointed:

"What's your race?"

"Do you speak Spanish?"

"What do you claim?"

I soon realized I was in a neighborhood where the most important questions focused on my race and my (presumed) gang affiliation. My combination of dark hair and eyes and light skin puzzled people in my new community. I was now in an agricultural town composed of Mexican immigrant parents and their American-born children. No one was sure of my ethnicity, and it was now an issue. I didn't know how to respond.

I wanted to play it safe. Get good grades. Respect my teachers. Be nice to other kids. How could that go wrong?

"Schoolboy!"

"Only white kids care about homework, loser."

"Why do you read so much? Only loners read books."

I soon realized that getting good grades and answering questions in class were *not* the way to be accepted. And even when it didn't concern my academics, I was called "fat," "four-eyes," "nerd"—you know the drill. The verbal taunts were easy to ignore at first, but then the physical bullying started; slaps, shoves, being spit on, getting hit with rocks, having my backpack stolen and thrown over a fence. It only took a year in California for me to realize that being chubby, wearing glasses, and not "claiming" gang affiliation or "ethnic solidarity" was going to get me brutalized.

I really wanted friends. Kids loved playing basketball at recess. I wasn't athletic—not even close . . . but what did I have to lose? One day I put myself into a game. No one objected. Everything was great until the teacher on yard duty blew her whistle.

"Freeze!" she screamed.

We were expected to stop what we were doing until she said to relax. But the tallest kid in our group, Jair, kept moving. The teacher saw him and sentenced us all to detention.

In a moment of bravery (or stupidity), I looked up at him and yelled, "You can't play with us anymore!"

The fist to my face was swift. I fell to my knees on the asphalt.

Various boys ran up to watch the spectacle and hollered, "Kick his ass, Chris, kick his ass!"

"Right," I thought. "He's six feet tall."

Little did I know Jair would become my first friend in California.

Jair's parents were never home, and his house was a mess. He had no food in the pantry and he never seemed to shower. He threw a chair at a teacher once.

He never apologized for punching me, but after I got to know him, I understood. He may have been of the dominant ethnicity in this little agricultural town, but he was too tall, didn't talk enough, and didn't say the right things when he did. I'd later learn that he had a dark past.

One day three boys near a trailer park started screaming at him, "You stink! Why don't you take a shower?"

They kept teasing him until he snapped. I watched in amazement as he beat all three of them up. In his rage-filled retribution, I saw a model for what my life was to become in California—punch first, ask questions later. Gangbanging in my new home was at an all-time high back then. No internet, no cell phones—but plenty of shootings, stabbings, robberies, and assaults. A "normal childhood" was not an option. Playing by the rules of the street was the only option.

Jair and I stayed friends until my freshman year of high school. He eventually moved to another state, but not before he shared stories with me of getting abused by male family members. Eventually his size allowed him to beat one of them up, but could that heal the psychological scars? Once he shared his stories with me, I realized why we had come together. We both had serious trauma and didn't know how to deal with it in a healthy way. Lost people sometimes cling to one another when they feel abandoned.

These days there's considerable discussion about bullying. This is fantastic for the current school-age generation, but that level of awareness didn't exist when I was growing up. I never had a teacher, administrator, or mentor who cared about the nightmare I endured in California's public schools. Advice like "ignore the bully" or "tell the principal" was as empty as it sounded. Kids like me suffered deeply. We suffered for caring about grades, suffered when we read books at recess, and got called "soft" because we cared more about homework than smoking meth behind the supermarket or "putting in work" for a gang. I look back on the circumstances in which I grew up and am amazed that I managed to survive.

I thirsted for a physical space where I could feel safe. I found this in my high school library. I had taken up guitar, and being in a band kept me busy, at least after school. Lunch, though . . . well . . . I went to the library and helped staff organize the card catalog (remember those?). Doing so gave me a purpose other than being that kid who sat by himself every day.

In my sophomore year, I got hit by a truck. The library became a physical and mental hideout while I learned how to walk again. Things were quiet there. It was the only place where adults smiled at me instead of scowling.

In my junior year, my band was wildly popular, and for once, so was I. The library seemed a distant memory, and I stopped going there every day. I had friends now. I felt like I didn't have to hide from other kids.

In my senior year, the band broke up over a girl. All the popular kids turned their backs on me again. No more band, no more friends.

I started college but was not passionate about it. A girl I had a crush on died in an earthquake. I almost ran off to Pennsylvania to live on a Hare Krishna commune. I was apathetic. I became a punk rock and hardcore kid, and when those genres weren't loud enough, I became a metalhead.

Life became all about heavy metal—I had stopped caring about grades. Class was just an interlude between jam sessions and playing shows. The new band I was in was famous locally, and it was surreal to leave a venue and be pulled aside by fans who talked about how "extreme" (loud) we were.

I played metal but listened to Coltrane and Miles Davis in my off time. I still couldn't escape the anti-intellectuals in the local metal scene, those people who make fun of you for making good grades like that's some sort of bad thing.

"What Do You Mean You Listen to Jazz? That's Not *Metal*, Bro."

Good thing no one realized I was mellowing out and starting to play acoustic guitar. The vocalist in my band and I had it out, and I was gone from the band. No matter. I needed softness. Positivity. Metal was cathartic, but I didn't want to feel numb anymore. I started playing quiet folk music in my room and taking college seriously again.

About halfway through my undergrad, I was in a course that required me to do a form of community service called "service learning." The idea was to have a more symbiotic relationship with a work site than just "here for two weeks, then gone forever." I started going to a library in nearby Castroville a few times a week. Kids who needed help with homework would sit with me for hours and we could connect—not just as mentor and student, but as friends. One kid used to look at my steel-toe boots and ask, "Are you a fireman?"

The library was a place where anybody could come and receive an equal level of respect, quiet, and educational opportunity. I was skeptical. What could a jaded metalhead like me get from a public library? I had always seen the library as one thing—an escape from bullies. I had never seen it as a place of respect or opportunity.

I connected with another student who was also doing her service learning there, and we took to sitting out front telling stories and laughing after our shifts were over. My gloomy outlook on life was lifting, ever so slightly.

This mood boost was enough to send me into overdrive during my last two years of college, and I graduated *magna cum laude* with distinction in my major—journalism. I felt on top of the world, and my family was proud.

After the glow wore off, I realized I needed a job. I applied anywhere I could think of: Forest Service, computer technician, newspaper intern. I didn't get an interview for any of them other than the newsroom. A grizzled reporter told me what a horrible profession journalism was. How the pay would level off quickly. How I would stagnate. He scared me off.

I started eating a bag of marshmallows every day and put on over twenty pounds. Emotional eating was a bad habit I'd sometimes had as a kid, but not to this level. I felt stuck.

"Help Wanted at the Gonzales Library"

This was 2005—still the days of help-wanted ads in newspapers. I called the number, got a tour and interview, and soon I was working fifteen hours a week at a tiny rural library in Gonzales, California. I started really finding my groove in library work. But many staff members came and went, often saying they had "big opportunities" elsewhere (usually in a city).

Too country for them, I thought with a chuckle. I had never left my small-town roots.

In early 2017, I had the opportunity to interview to be a branch manager at the branch I had been working in for over a decade. I never assumed it was owed to me. I took the interview process very seriously and put my heart into every answer. I received the offer in April 2017.

I thought about all the years I had spent immersing myself in library life, and I was determined to humbly take the helm and always evolve and improve in my profession. I did, however, need a focus. I was never a tech guru. My writing and speaking skills were strong, but what was my bailiwick?

People.

I had learned how to read when people felt depressed, lost, or hopeless.

Most of my life I had felt depressed, lost, and hopeless. Takes one to know one.

People come to libraries for a multitude of reasons. It is common to hear about the public attending free programs or joining book clubs. It isn't so common to hear about those who come in because they want a safe place to spend a moment, or a sliver of small talk and a smile from library staff.

It is a gift to be part of a community. In the small community I serve, I see a lot of love. I also see a lot of people who are hurting and who feel frustrated with their lives. In many of them, I see the person I once was. This helps me relate. Young men out here see their only "legitimate" job options as packing vegetables in a packing plant or driving big-rig trucks for produce companies. These are honest jobs, but it makes me sad that other types of jobs, especially those that are more mind than body, are seen as out of reach.

I offer my patrons this: a listening ear, a friend, someone you can ask almost anything and get a sincere answer, someone who will smile and laugh with you when you graduate college or get married, someone who will show genuine sympathy when you lose a loved one. My patrons often let me know—verbally or not—that I've touched their lives.

I could easily agonize over my difficult childhood and expect lifelong sympathy. It still is hard at times. But I'm not a fatalist, and certainly no nihilist. I've seen how overcoming adversity can make a person very, very strong. I've also seen how love and decency can melt some of the negativity in people's lives. A free public library, simple and humble, and its staff, caring and compassionate, can be a wonderful place. Will any of us become millionaires? Probably not, but we have the priceless gift of community, decency, and respect. These things can't be bought or sold. Sometimes they only become evident after years of soul-searching. They became evident to me in the library.

4

Fire and Flood, Philippe Petit, and a Pork Chop

The Story of the Phoenicia Library

~ REBEKKAH SMITH ALDRICH ~

Believe marvels exist around you, inside others, within yourself . . .
—**Philippe Petit**, *Cheating the Impossible: Ideas and Recipes from a Rebellious High-Wire Artist*

This is the story of a library that once was, then wasn't, then burned, then flooded, then got sued (twice), and then rose from the ashes both literally and figuratively. This is a story I keep close to my heart, that I turn to when I am feeling discouraged about the world around me. I hope it makes you smile and warms your heart and reminds you that no matter how bad things seem, there is always hope.

"FIRE GUTS LIBRARY," read the headline of the March 20, 2011, issue of the *Daily Freeman*. The words felt like a punch, and I winced as I read them. But at least it was a sign I was out of the stupor I'd been in since Judith

19

Singer, the board president of the Phoenicia Library, had called me the day before—with the sound of fire engines in the background—to tell me their library was on fire.

I am a consultant at a cooperative, regional library system in upstate New York. For twenty years, my job has been to assist our member libraries as they work to evolve to meet the needs of their communities, creating sustainable organizations that are resilient and responsive. But a fire of this magnitude? This was a first.

"Would you come and help us?" asked Judith. "Absolutely," I said confidently, feeling like a complete fraud. I had no idea how to help them. I didn't feel prepared to help them one bit, but I still got in my car and made the trek out to Phoenicia, a hamlet of 309 people, the largest community in the town of Shandaken in Ulster County, New York. It's one of my favorite drives, and destinations, in our region, "nestled in the gateway of the magnificent Catskill Forest Preserve"; the views are lovely, the cell phone service is nonexistent, and the people, what to say about the people?

In a 2002 article in the *New York Times*, Claudia Rowe described Phoenicia as "a quirky amalgam of dyed-in-the-wool lifers, artistic souls, leather-clad bikers, and solitary curmudgeons who get along, perhaps because they agree that it is worth forgoing amenities like laundromats and malls for peace and quiet." This is an apt description of those I have had the privilege of meeting through my work with this library.

The Phoenicia Library has had its ups and downs. In 1901, the library received its provisional charter from the state. However, in 1918, the librarian, Mrs. Ralph Longyear, reported that no new books had been purchased since 1912, and their borrower base of fifty people had dwindled down to "two or three a week." "The people of Phoenicia are not interested in a Library to the extent of supporting it with money," wrote Mrs. Longyear, "and also they do not care to patronize it." After a correspondence with Mrs. Longyear, the state recommended the revocation of the library's charter. The collection, valued at $483, was turned over to the school district.

In 1959, the citizens of the hamlet decided it was time to have an official library again. In their application to the state—the Phoenicia Library Association, run by ten "volunteer librarians" overseeing a collection of more than 2,800 books with "spotty" subject coverage—we can see evidence of the growing population of Phoenicia, spurred by both the expansion of IBM's facilities to the nearby city of Kingston and the growth of the resort community in the locality. The state consultant's report notes both discouraging and encouraging features:

Discouraging features:
1. Volunteer help
2. Book collection meager

Encouraging features:
1. Entire community's enthusiasm over library
2. Town support assured
3. Good publicity
4. Excellent equipment
5. Interest in cooperative library system

By 1964, a state inspection noted that the library was doing well, and the library's trustees were "surely interested and enthusiastic about the library" and were "working hard for its support." Despite serving a population less than the minimum the state would normally consider necessary to support adequate public library service, the enthusiasm of the library's trustees and the statistical growth of the previous five years convinced the state that this was a viable library, and so it granted their absolute charter.

For the fifty-five years since then, the Phoenicia Library has held its own, proving the state right.

Perhaps it is the visual image of "books burning" that correlates to "book burnings"—a ritual destruction of books by fire carried out in a public setting as a form of cultural censorship—that makes a library fire much worse in my mind than just your average structural fire. The visceral reaction to books burning is real; it's the fear that our history and the knowledge of our civilization will be compromised. Even in a small, rural library whose collection was primarily popular reading materials that could be found in just about any library in America, we find a unique corner of our collective knowledge, the Jerry Bartlett Memorial Angling Collection.

"Fire is the test of gold; adversity, of strong men."
–SENECA

"The Catskills is famous as the place where fly fishing began in North America. As early as the 1830s Phoenicia is distinguished for having the first boarding house that catered to fishermen. The Jerry Bartlett Memorial Angling Collection at the Phoenicia Library celebrates Catskill angling history and traditions with an extensive collection of books about fishing and fly tying, as well as historical memorabilia, artworks, archives, and other resources. The special collection opened in 1996 in memory of Jerry Bartlett (1939-1995) a conservationist and tireless advocate for the cold water fisheries of the Catskill Mountains."

–PHOENICIA LIBRARY,
http://phoenicialibrary.org/jerry-bartlett-angling-collection/

People cannot be replaced. But their wisdom, acquired and honed over a lifetime, can be captured in their writings. A library is often described as a temple to that wisdom, connecting citizens with the knowledge, experience, and education we need to expand our understanding of the world around us, as well as our efforts to improve that world.

In each corner of our world, we find uniqueness worthy of preservation. Sometimes that uniqueness takes the form of the written word, a "Catskill-style" floating fly, or the volunteer spirit that creates community out of adversity.

In the aftermath of the electrical fire at the Phoenicia Library on the morning of March 19, 2011, the library's director, Tracy Priest, and the board of trustees found themselves the recipients of much goodwill. Within a week of the fire, a temporary location to create a library facility had been secured and spruced up. Boxes and boxes of book donations arrived, computers were donated, and regular patrons began showing up, accessing library services provided by a team of library staff and volunteers who were still reeling from the shock of the fire. An upstairs room at 9 Ava Maria Drive, opposite the post office in Phoenicia, had even been painted and decorated to reestablish the Bartlett Angling Collection, and a call for books, furniture, and angling artifacts related to Esopus Creek and nearby streams had been issued. It was, in the words of Tracy Priest, "a bare-bones operation," with books being lent on the honor system at first because the barcodes had been destroyed in the fire.

The town supervisor hinted that the new location could be permanent, noting that it was larger than the original building. Board President Judith Singer was cautious about confirming this, noting that the board was initially at odds over where to locate the new building, but wherever it would end up, "we're going to do our best to replicate the warm, welcoming atmosphere the library has always offered. That's key to the Phoenicia Library."

The library's leadership was incredibly busy managing a deluge of book donations, handling questions about the future of the library, and doing their best to create a library service center that helped people feel that their library had not been lost. The indomitable human spirit was on display both among the community members who were stepping up from all over town to help and among the dedicated and hard-working trustees.

As I began meeting with the board to chart a course forward, we contended with challenging issues: Should they seek a new location? Was it financially responsible to build on the original Main Street footprint, which lies on a floodplain? Where would the money to build come from? As an association library in New York, they didn't have the capacity to bond for a new facility. Any funds would have to be sought from private donors, legislators, and grant-makers—a long haul for a small library in a small community that needed to build a facility and collection from the ground up.

It quickly became clear that there was an emotional commitment to remain a Main Street anchor. Main Street is in a floodplain, and the library building had flooded in the past. During an interview with library trustee Beth Waterman, she reminisced about the flood that once brought four feet of water to the center of the hamlet: "There were fish swimming down Main Street!" Choosing to remain in the location they had inhabited before the fire would not be without controversy, but they were committed. While many residents were drawn to Phoenicia and the surrounding area for the ability to live quietly in nature, the desire for human connection and neighborly interactions is manifested on Main Street. The library's leadership knew that to be viable, they needed to remain a staple of Main Street life. Their strength as a community asset before the fire was entwined with the fact that they had never been just a building with books in it; they have always been a community meeting space, a place for people to gather and socialize with one another.

During my first visit to the Phoenicia Library, when I began working for the Mid-Hudson Library System in 1998, I was struck by the fact that it was unlike any other library I had ever visited before. It was, to be blunt, run-down, and there were far too many books in the space, but it was homey and inviting. As I sat primly in a weird green armchair waiting for the director, two people entered the building with their dogs. The dogs seemed enormous to me in that small library. One was, in fact, a rather large Newfoundland, and the other was a chocolate brown Labrador retriever. They made a circuit, sniffing out the corners and stacks, making sure that all was as it should be. And then they sat in front of me, as if waiting for something. I looked up, unsure of what was going on. Were these dogs even *allowed* in the library? Should I give in and pet them? The owner of the Newfoundland cheerfully informed me that I was in the dogs' seat. I dutifully got up and they jostled each other, the Lab winning the seat in the armchair, standing on it, circling, and then settling in, head on the armrest, front legs dangling off the front of the chair. I sat in the next chair over, a hard-backed dining room chair. The Newfoundland cheerily sat on my feet and looked up hopefully, compelling me to pet him. The dogs' owners casually sat down across from each other, propping their feet up on the coffee table, sipping coffee from to-go cups they'd gotten from Sweet Sue's across the street, and proceeded to catch up on the week's gossip in town. It was like a neighborhood living room. I settled in, and a strange sense of relaxation and warmth spread through me. I liked this even though I knew, as a library consultant, that I should be appalled. Feet on the furniture? Dogs in the library! As I drove home later in the day, I laughed ruefully to myself because, honestly, I couldn't wait to go back.

Once the decision to stay on Main Street was made, we rolled up our sleeves to make it happen. I had recently passed the exam to be a Leadership in Energy and Environmental Design Accredited Professional (LEED AP), and I was anxious to influence local library boards to choose sustainable design when they had the opportunity to do so. I am emphatically committed to the idea that sustainable design is essential to the future of creating viable libraries that want to demonstrate their care and concern for both library workers and patrons. I had been unsuccessful thus far in convincing any library board that this was a good idea, though. Myths about the price tag on sustainable design were a huge obstacle to my ability to make my case. Though the Phoenicia Library's board members didn't need much of a sales pitch from me, they got one anyway. They quickly prioritized an energy-efficient building built by local craftspeople with local resources. A local builder emerged, offering to help rebuild the library on its original footprint at a greatly reduced fee for his services. This builder spent much of his time designing and constructing incredibly beautiful and expensive homes for second-home owners from New York City, but he was excited about a new certification he had in Passive House design, a standard for constructing energy-efficient buildings. And as a local resident, he wanted to see his local library rebuilt. Once he was able to demonstrate that the increased costs to use Passive Design would be paid back by the energy savings achieved, and he agreed to the board's goals for energy efficiency, flood-proofing, and their desire to reuse materials and "buy local," the library board decided to work with him. We were on our way. Or so we thought.

Five months after the fire, Hurricane Irene hit Phoenicia. I had never considered the Catskill Mountains an area vulnerable to hurricanes, but we all learned an important lesson in August 2011 when Irene, one of the top ten worst catastrophes to ever hit the United Sates, arrived. Houses were washed away. Cement bridges collapsed, and Phoenicia's Main Street flooded for the third time in its history. With impassable roads and a critical bridge damaged, the residents were literally cut off from the world in the aftermath of Irene, and many residents were in desperate need of assistance.

The library's Facebook page became a go-to source for local information in the aftermath, as the staff amplified messages from the town and emergency service officials about road closures, water contamination, and boiled-water advisories; information about where to get sand and shovels; calls for help for volunteers to pump out basements; and how to file for federal assistance. This "town crier" role brought many new residents to the library's social media presence, and the community-centric role the library played in those days and weeks after the flooding were, in a way, a big signal to the community that the fire had knocked the library down, but not out. The library was a connector, providing a community service in the midst of its own tragedy.

The flood oddly spared the library's burnt-out location on Main Street, with floodwaters rising just to the top of the foundation, but not damaging the structure any further.

From that moment on, I feel that the fate of the town and the library shifted. The townspeople were galvanized by the two catastrophes that had befallen them in the form of the fire and the flood. The board went full speed ahead with their plans to rebuild on Main Street, working with the Federal Emergency Management Agency to ensure the new facility would be flood-proof. Fundraising kicked into high gear, and supporters came out of the woodwork to help the board bring their vision to life.

Mama's Boy Market Café sponsored a bake-off to raise funds. A local celebrity couple, the songwriter Holly George-Warren and the musician Uncle Rock (aka Robert Burke Warren), with a lot of help from their friends, organized a benefit concert featuring musicians like punk rocker Tommy Ramone, Levon Helm's Ramble Band, and even opera singers! A child brought seven dollars into the temporary space to donate to the rebuilding fund. The library director and board worked feverishly to write grants, speak with prospective donors, and say yes to every offer of assistance.

In September 2011, the magazine *Budget Travel* named Phoenicia one of the "Coolest Small Towns in America." The feature article noted: "Phoenicia may look like a one-street river town sandwiched between hills in New York's Catskills—it does a wicked tubing business in the summer—but it's got a bookish cosmopolitan vibe in its soul."

Was this the upswing we had all been hoping for?

In May 2012, Library Director Tracy Priest made a career move to be closer to home, and former library trustee Elizabeth (Liz) Potter stepped up as the new library director. Liz began her tenure as director just as a new challenge faced the library—two lawsuits. Neighbors on both sides of the library's Main Street location sued the town and the library, challenging technicalities in the zoning process. Neither the library nor the town had the money to fight the lawsuits, and a public relations campaign was piled on top of the library's capital campaign efforts. This period was marked by impassioned speeches at town board meetings, neighbors arguing on the sidewalk in front of the properties, and a heartbreaking amount of energy diverted away from the rebuilding effort.

"The long-suffering Phoenicia Library needs more help," read the opening line of an October 2012 article in the *Daily Freeman*. "This time though, it's more about moral support than the usual fundraising requests . . ."

Eventually the board got through this new crisis, but not without some bruises. With building permits finally in place, construction could begin, but they still needed a considerable chunk of money to bring the project to life. The board *indefatigably* continued on and organized a formal capital campaign kickoff event with a special guest whose name they kept under wraps, drumming up excitement about the mysterious guest. In complete Phoenicia fashion—unexpected, quirky, and imperfectly perfect—the speaker at the event turned out to be Philippe Petit, the French high-wire artist who is best known for his high-wire walk between the Twin Towers of the World Trade Center in New York City in 1974. Library Director Liz Potter, when reminiscing about the event, noted that he couldn't have been a more perfect speaker for the event because "he did the impossible in his life, and that's what the library's leadership was doing as well." Against all odds, the library's director and board were committed to bringing a library worthy of the community back to Main Street.

Grant-writing continued, generous donors emerged, and "coins, small bills, and large checks" were put into big glass jars. Small fundraising events like a dance party, a ukulele concert, and "Bing + Barbecue + Bourbon," which actually served more as "friendraising" family-style events than as money-makers, coaxed residents out of their homes and into local establishments like the Peekamoose Restaurant and Tap Room. Then the artisans arrived: a custom circulation desk was designed and built by a local woodworker, a $30,000 value, at no cost to the library; furniture from the former Bartlett room was painstakingly refinished by another local craftsman, at no cost to the library; and lighting experts who had just come off a job lighting the Magna Carta exhibit in Washington, D.C., came to work on the project, at a greatly reduced cost to the library.

Construction commenced in September 2013 and was completed on schedule, enabling the rebuilt library to reopen on January 1, 2015. The result is a library that was designed around people, not stuff. The new building is in fact the first Passive House–designed library in the United States. This means that they doubled the square footage of the former facility yet cut energy bills by 85 percent, saving $6,800 annually. The interior is 100 percent compliant with the Americans with Disabilities Act and boasts, yes boasts, a well thought-out collection that is a third *smaller* than the former collection but which has enjoyed enormous increases in circulation statistics—up 51 percent in the first year and, on average, 8 percent annually since then. The meeting room can host 30 programs a month, rather than 30 a year as was previously the case, and has yielded a 180 percent increase in program attendance. And yes, the re-created Jerry Bartlett Angling Collection has its very own room. It is no surprise that the library won the 2016 Building of the Year award from the New York Library Association.

"What we gained is so much more than what we lost," says trustee Beth Waterman, and she wasn't talking about the square footage. When I asked Beth what stood out to her most about the grand reopening ceremony, she said, "All my friends were there."

The grand reopening ceremony was something to behold; a simple ceremony with the usual speeches from legislators, library trustees, donors . . . and some library consultant named Rebekkah. However, there was not a dry eye in the house by the time the ribbon was cut. That community had *endured* to get to that moment. They had pulled together with purpose, determination, and frankly, love for one another. That ceremony was a celebration of what humans can do when they decide they care enough about one another to work together and truly be a community.

Since opening in its new location, the library has continued its role as a connector, hosting local authors and musicians and casting a warm glow onto Main Street through the large picture window that provides a view into Phoenicia's new living room. The library has maintained its town crier role, most recently alerting residents to lost pets in town. In 2018, the library held a ceremony to celebrate the reunion of Lucas "the Miracle Dog" with his owner. Lucas had been reported missing and, thanks to the library getting the word out, the town sprang into action searching for him in the mountains around town. After a week, a neighbor spotted Lucas and lured him to their home with a pork chop. The story is now legend, and the library hosted an event to enable residents to meet Lucas and his family, to "hear his tale of woe," and to "relive the famous 'pork chop' reunification." The photos of the event convey the pure joy that Lucas and his family were experiencing and the goodwill of a community pleased for their neighbor.

What is life without the joy of human connection? What is life without care and concern for others? The story and continuing legacy of this library always serve to remind me that there is so much good in the world, and that what seems impossible is absolutely possible when we work together.

What's Your Superpower?

~ TOM BRUNO ~

t's about half an hour until closing time at the library on a Friday afternoon, and we're busy as usual. Even though we changed our hours last July, people still come in thinking they have time to spare, only to realize that we close at 2:00 p.m., and then panic quickly ensues. As I field a steady stream of patrons needing help with the photocopier—it's on the fritz again, naturally, even though we just had it serviced the other week—or hoping to buy refuse tickets for the Town Dump so they can get some weekend yardwork done, I am flagged down by a tall, lanky man who says he needs some help uploading some documents. I show him to the computer workstation where we have a flatbed scanner attached and start walking him through the process.

"Sorry to be a bother," he apologizes as I show him how the scanner works. "I'm just no good with technology."

"No need to apologize," I tell him. "That's what we're here for."

I work at a small public library in a town in southwestern Connecticut, about seventy miles from New York City. Our community is a mixture of professionals drawn by affordable housing prices who commute to the city or who work in the many businesses located in Lower Fairfield County, and locals with roots stretching back generations who have lived here since the area was mostly rural and farmland. Although in many respects this is an almost stereotypical sleepy New England town, owing to our library's inviting spaces, ample parking, and (most importantly) our unrestricted computers, we often get a lot of patrons from the neighboring towns and the nearby city of Bridgeport.

The man tells me that he has been driving for a ride-share service, picking up passengers and making food deliveries all over this half of Connecticut and New York City. He does most of his business overnight, when the competition is less cutthroat.

"I just got another job with a different ride-sharing service," he explains. "They need my license, registration, and a photo so I can start driving for them, but I can't make heads or tails of their website."

I smile reassuringly. "Not a problem. I can help you with that as well."

Technology help is a lot of what we do here at the reference desk. People come in feeling more or less bewildered by the digital world and its ever-changing requirements and demands. This is especially true for those who don't have computers or the internet at home. As society moves increasingly to an online-only world, just to apply for a job at a supermarket you need to create an online account on the company's website, upload your resume, and take a forty-question psychological profile test. Thus, a substantial portion of the population is suddenly finding that they are at the mercy of the computer when before they at least had the luxury of pretending to ignore it.

The supermarket example is fresh in my mind because I recently helped someone apply for a job as a restocking clerk. He was a younger man with special needs who had tried to apply on-site at the store but was directed to the internet, so he came to us because he knew we'd help him. As it turns out, this is a recurring theme that I hear when I sit down with people and help them with their technology questions. "You actually listen," one elderly woman told me as I helped her try to figure out how to manage the pictures on her iPhone during one of my drop-in Tech Help Tuesday sessions, which have proven very popular with the community. The woman continued, "The people at the store couldn't get rid of me fast enough."

I think about how our library is an anomaly in this regard. Even though most of American society is now based on the so-called "service economy," the old industrial factory mindset is still very much in charge in the workplace. Get the customers in, get them out. The longer it takes to resolve a problem, the worse your performance numbers will look, so ironically, the customers who come in with the most difficult problems are the ones who are most likely to end up walking away disappointed, frustrated, or angry.

Here at our library, though, we don't make a patron feel unwelcome because they need help; even before technology became one of our specialties, trouble-shooting was always our business. People would come to us with questions, and we would do our best to figure out the answer. Rather than shooing away patrons who have thorny problems, librarians in fact relish the challenge of solving the unsolvable. Sure, we count our transactions just like any other service desk, but people always come before numbers. I've yet to work at a library service desk where employees are chastised for taking too long to help someone.

Nevertheless, the tall, lanky man I'm helping feels the need to apologize again, especially as he sees people starting to queue up at the reference desk. "Sorry, I should have come sooner. I didn't realize there would be such a rush!"

"Not to worry, really." I let the people at the desk know I'll be right with them, as I'm just finishing scanning the last of the documents; they nod understandingly. Then I realize there's a problem: the documents are in the wrong format. Our scanner is set up to automatically convert everything to PDF files because that's the format that most people need when they are scanning documents, but this company's website wants all of the documents uploaded as images, for some reason.

Crap. This is going to take longer than I thought. I'm about to excuse myself for a moment so that I can help the people in line when the circulation supervisor comes to my rescue. My coworkers are always there in a pinch to help—it's one of the things that I love about working here. Perhaps it's a cliché to say it takes a village, but library work often feels exactly like that. Although as the reference librarian, I'm supposed to be the person who knows all the answers, in truth I'm just the person who knows where to go and who to ask to get those answers. At its heart, the library is a collaborative effort, and I am grateful to be part of a team where everyone is willing and able to help.

Because the scanner's not an option, I decide instead to take pictures of the documents we need with my phone and e-mail them to the man so we can download them to the computer and then upload them to the website. It's a clunky workaround, to be sure, but at least it's a solution. There's a strong sense of "You Can't Get There from Here" in trying to solve many of the technology problems that our patrons bring to the library because each online service or company's web page makes its own peculiar demands of people who are struggling simply with how to use their smartphones or log into their e-mail.

We librarians like to talk a lot about the "digital divide" as if there are two clearly delineated groups of people—those who have online access and are fluent in technology, and those who are not—but in truth the divide is more like a series of swiftly moving and unpredictable barriers that can trip up virtually anyone. Just the other day, I had to explain the difference between a PDF and a JPEG to a Zoomer fresh out of high school who was struggling to print an image from his phone, so even the supposed digital natives are not immune to the demands of this technological rat race. In fact, the generations accustomed to everything working like magic are sometimes the most flummoxed when the underlying technology actually does break down.

"How do you have time to keep on top of all this stuff?" a patron once asked me as I helped her make some formatting changes to a document in Microsoft Word. While she was by no means a stranger to computers, she was nonetheless exasperated by having to figure out how to do everything all over again with each successive version of the software. I shrugged and considered her question. While I've always been adept at figuring out technology, I've never really considered myself to be a computer person. But then it hit me: I can keep up with this stuff because it's my job to keep up. Not everyone has the luxury of getting paid to stay current with the latest technological advances.

Another thing about assisting library patrons with technology is being able to tell when somebody wants to learn and when someone just needs what they need to go about their business. We like to share knowledge and we love to teach people how to fish, but sometimes a patron just wants a box of frozen fish sticks because it's late in the day already and they're starving. While there are a few people out there who might want to understand the technological obstacles that are preventing them from, say, printing the record of a text conversation off of their phone, most of them just want the printouts.

[Side note: If someone actually does figure out how to easily print directly from a mobile device to a public printer, they will make a small fortune with the library community. So get to it, already!]

I remember one woman in the library; her eyes were red from crying and she was visibly shaking as she tried to do something on the computer—but she kept getting stuck on something, so I approached her and asked her if she needed help. She was trying to download and print out some legal forms, and I could tell without prying that it involved something extremely unpleasant, which explained why even the tiniest setback was almost too much for her to deal with. She was almost in a state of disbelief that I was willing to sit down with her and make sure she was able to get through the entire process, and I did my best to reassure her when we did hit a couple of snags along the way that I wasn't going to leave until she had what she needed. While there was nothing I could do about her current legal predicament, I was at least able to take her mind off figuring out how to handle all of the paperwork. Sometimes every little bit helps.

As I help the tall, lanky man get his documents out of his e-mail and uploaded to the ride-share company's website at long last, I know that this is another one of those instances where delivering the goods is the most important thing I can do at the moment. He just needs my help right now, and he is very grateful for my time and assistance.

"I was hoping you'd be here," he says to me as I'm finishing up the process. "I don't know if you remember, but the last time I was here you helped me fill out an application for a different job."

I'm trying to recall helping him. I vaguely remember him from several weeks ago when I was working a Saturday shift. The online application form was giving him trouble, so he called me over and I helped him finish it before it timed out on him.

"Well, I just wanted to let you know that I got that job you helped me apply for."

"Oh, that's awesome!" I say. When you assist someone at the reference desk, you're never quite sure how it all turned out. As librarians, we are often privy to just a tiny sliver of our patrons' lives, and we can only hope that the book we recommended or the answer we provided—or, in this case, the help we gave—was actually what they needed. So I'm genuinely pleased to hear that this man landed a job through my efforts, but I was absolutely floored by what he said next.

"As a matter of fact, because I could document my income from that job, I was able to avoid foreclosure on my house."

I look up from the computer. Is it my imagination, or has my heart stopped? As I fight back tears, I try to say something appropriate in response, but the words fail me at that moment.

"Yeah," he says, reading my reaction. He looks a little misty-eyed himself.

My tongue finally helps me out and I stammer, "I—I'm so happy to hear that."

The man nods. "You really helped me out of a jam that day."

As I think back to that moment, I am humbled by both its ordinariness and its importance. There was no way of knowing that the man I was helping was literally one paycheck away from homelessness. What if I had brushed him off as a cranky old man who was afraid of technology instead of being patient with him? What if I had rushed him through the job application process because I was under the gun to finish up with him already and get to the next patron, so I wouldn't get disciplined for taking too much time? There are a million ways that I could have been less helpful to that man, had I been working anywhere else but a library.

Libraries are made of these moments. Some of them are life-altering like this particular instance, but even when they aren't, we are improving lives and making the world a slightly better place through our efforts. That is why libraries are essential. In many communities, we are one of the last places left that takes all comers and doesn't have an angle. As the American social safety net erodes on the national, state, county, and local levels, the public library has become a last refuge for many who truly have no other place to go. While some librarians grumble about having to take on the mantle of social worker in addition to their other job duties, on a fundamental level librarianship has always embraced the notion of social responsibility. Even in a moderately well-off community such as the one in which I work, there are people who need the library in order to live: not just the man looking for a job, but the immigration lawyer whose printer isn't working and who needs a quiet meeting space to consult confidentially with her clients; the artist without a computer who needs help submitting her work online for a show; and the mother who can't make sense of how to fill out her daughter's college medical forms so she can play soccer in the fall.

Sure, libraries are still about books, e-books, and other kinds of resources. But we're also about understanding, patience, and compassion. Often the work we do manifests itself in the form of recommending a book, finding the answer to a question, or troubleshooting an issue with technology, but sometimes it just consists of listening to someone and treating them with empathy as a fellow human being. In a world that seems increasingly impersonal and impatient, libraries are warm and inviting spaces where time isn't necessarily money, and the bottom line isn't the only thing that matters.

In spite of this, libraries and librarians don't always get the recognition they deserve from a public that doesn't read like they used to and thinks that everything is on the internet. But every now and then someone will praise librarians in a magazine or newspaper article, or in a post on social media. The renowned author Neil Gaiman, a great champion of libraries, famously said, "Google can bring you back 100,000 answers, a librarian can bring you back the right one." Susan Orleans, author of *The Library Book*, has even declared that librarians are superheroes. If librarians are in fact superheroes, I'd like to think our superpower would be actually giving a shit when nobody else does.

My name is Tom. I am a librarian, and I totally give a shit.

Me and the Library Dog

~ MELISSA M. POWELL ~

F or ten years, I had my own library consulting business. I mostly did project management and staff training, usually involving cataloging. Many of my clients were "accidental librarians"—those librarians who hadn't planned on being a librarian and didn't go to library school yet were passionate about the profession. I came in as the "expert," though I usually learned as much as I taught. These jobs often served to renew my own passion for library work. It is very inspiring to see people find their "inner librarian" and do a lot with a little because of their love of libraries and the people who use them.

One of my last and most rewarding jobs as a consultant was automating a residential high school's library in the mountains. The library was becoming a branch of the local public library district so that the high school could offer its students a more modern library experience, as well as share its unique collection with the residents of the town. This turned out to be the job that was completely in line with why I became a librarian in the first place.

The school itself fit the library philosophy of serving all by offering tuition-free, holistic education to teens who were in situations that kept them from thriving and learning. They were not in positive situations, yet they wanted to learn. The faculty taught by engaging the students in creative and practical ways, including outdoor education, combined science and art classes, and other creative ways to stimulate the mind for better learning.

The project itself was pretty straightforward and was similar to many I had already done: weed the existing collection, catalog and process what was left, and add the collection to the existing public library database. We had summer break, when the students were not on campus, to get this done.

The library staff consisted of one accidental librarian, who was also the art teacher, and one very cute dog.

My first meeting with the librarian was very relaxed and positive. She, like many of the school staff, lived on the campus, so it was like visiting someone's home. Coffee, munchies, a dog at our feet; this was library work I could get used to!

The primary focus was the students and faculty: how could the library be more organized and less confusing or overwhelming for the students coming in? The library was already being used for studying and computer work, and the students could check out books. However, there was just no real system for finding the books or tracking them. The shelves were just crammed from end to end with a myriad of books, including multiple copies of the rebound paperbacks so popular in schools.

We discussed how to classify the collection. Because the students came from challenging backgrounds, the last thing they needed was more complications. The goal was less frustration and fewer barriers to getting information. We decided that a curriculum-based system would be best. By making the sections match the departments at the school, the students would have a more familiar system with which to work; they could make the connections to the things they were learning in the classroom. We also created a very simple Cuttering system comprised of the author's last name and the first word of the title; again, very simple and straightforward, easy for someone to remember going to the shelves, and really simple for reshelving the materials. This logical and practical classification system also made the job of classifying items easier for the current librarian and anyone coming in to take over the library in the future.

I went away very excited to plan the project, but also concerned about meeting our deadline. There were two of us and the dog, but she was a small dog, so reaching the shelves was difficult for her. We were obviously going to need more help.

The first challenge was to get more experienced library people involved. I had hired subcontractors before, but this time I was particularly interested in getting people who would understand the uniqueness of the school and the library. The local public library cataloger was already on board, so I advertised for two more people on a local forum. We found one experienced cataloger familiar with school cataloging who was looking for a challenge, and one local library staff member who was interested in learning copy cataloging. The latter was also interested in pursuing her library degree with an eye toward working with underserved populations. I followed my gut on this one and brought her on. It turned out to be a great decision.

When I returned to the school to go over the plan, the current librarian had already created the section labels. They were large, color-coded, bright, and easy to read. It was genius! Each section would be colorful and obvious. Leave it to an art teacher to see the value in bold colors you can see across the room. She didn't feel limited to what she could buy from a library supplier. Score one for the accidental librarian. No little dinky dots for her!

I was really getting excited about this job. The creative thinking and open-mindedness of everyone involved were invigorating.

Planning was done. Now it was time for the project to get started.

When we arrived at the library the first morning, there was not only coffee but volunteers. Faculty and staff from the school were excited to help in any way they could to make the library the best it could be for the students.

After introductions and a briefing, everyone was assigned their spots. The catalogers downloaded records, printed off call number labels, and added RFID tags to each book. They called out questions when they had them, and I ran over to help. The librarian continued weeding and packing books, discovering a beautiful core collection along the way. We all shared some of the fun books we came across.

The most fun was had by the volunteers who were putting on call number labels, colored labels, book covers, and so on. Faculty members laid "claim" to their sections and proudly made the sections their own. They were all fascinated by the amount of work that went into the creation of a library. They felt a kinship with the library.

We ate lunch together, sharing snacks and stories. The librarian pumped 1980s tunes from her computer, and we sang along. The library buzzed with energy and excitement, enhanced by the beautiful mountain scenery outside the windows. The library began to look organized, colorful, and ready for students.

The library dog supervised between naps in the sun.

By the end of the week, the team had made a considerable dent in the project, as well as christening the space with a creative and productive energy that was palpable. All that was left were a few more days of cleanup and original cataloging, which I would handle. Coming into the space to finish up, I could still feel that positive energy. I was invigorated, knowing these efforts would benefit the students in so many ways.

Summer ended and the students returned. I came for that first day, armed with doughnuts for the staff and faculty. The students came in excited to greet their favorite people and see the "new" library. The looks on their faces when they saw the colorful sections and neatly shelved books were exhilarating. They played with the online catalog and, most especially, the self-checkouts. "You don't need to be here when I check out a book? Cool!"

Everyone involved felt good about this project. I was especially proud to have been a part of it. To me, it embodied everything a library is about: community, access to information, and giving people a chance to better themselves. Sometimes, when I think that I'm making too big a deal out of it, I remind myself: libraries are important and integral to our lives, and if I, as a librarian, can help just one life become even a little bit better, and help a few more people have a little more opportunity, then I can take comfort in knowing I'm doing it right.

Me and the library dog. She's doing it right, too.

7

Miguel

~ YAGO CURA ~

The teens had their tutors, and the little ones had their readers, but when I started as an adult librarian at the Vernon Branch of the Los Angeles Public Library, one of the first things I noticed was an almost complete lack of programming for adults. I'm not talking about book clubs and tax preparation; I'm talking about health programs, like yoga classes, and finance symposia—you know, programs that educate, enrich, and elongate human life.

In the Central-Alameda neighborhood, there seemed to be a lack of programming, specifically for adults, maybe because what was needed was so much more than what adult programming alone could fix. I fought the pernicious belief that librarians did not have a prerogative to entice adults to come back or even enter our brick-and-mortar buildings—the place where the bookshelves are—because we had other fires that required our attention more urgently. Because of the incidents with addicts coming to our public restrooms to shoot meth or smoke crack cocaine, our staff had to expend a lot of time and energy on policing the restrooms. I mean, how could we really be expected to create and develop programming if we had grown adults, with all of their pathologies in tow, shooting up in our bathrooms?

If I am not mistaken, Miguel lived in Inglewood. But he came all the way to South Central Los Angeles on Tuesdays at 4:00 p.m. for my basic computer class. I had started the classes shortly after I started at the Vernon Branch, and I continued them throughout my tenure there. It was inspiring to think that the classes I was teaching were actually helping to fill a void and right a wrong. To me, for a student to come from Inglewood, they had to commit. And Miguel was nothing if not committed: he stood five foot eight but had the posture of a much taller man. And he attended my weekly classes for at least a year, which means that Miguel left the branch having learned at least fifty-two new things about computers and technology since he'd first come through the doors, and I am okay with that.

Maybe it was his neatly trimmed moustache and gold, wire-frame glasses, but he was always neat, *prolijo*, almost dapper. I never saw Miguel without a windbreaker and *mochila*, or backpack—all of it stamped with logos from mom-and-pop accounting firms like Del Valle Associates or enormous conglomerates like Verizon. In this respect, he dressed like a Latin American version of a North American youth, like the kids in the movie *The Sandlot*, if the movie had been set in Morelia or Matamoros instead of that nondescript American town in the movie. With a combover and his Verizon windbreaker, Miguel religiously attended my library computer class. For the class, we would block out one of the two islands of public-access computers so that all the patrons in the branch had just one island of ten computers to count on. In retrospect, it probably wasn't the most compassionate idea to cut off computer access for an hour to so many working-class people, but six or seven seniors routinely showed up, and that was enough to keep my bosses off my back.

I marketed and "sold" the class to Spanish-dominant senior citizens in South Central Los Angeles, and it worked like gangbusters. The classes were filling a need that many family members might not want to fulfill. It was like that maxim in *Field of Dreams*: "If you build it, they will come." My bosses let me commandeer an island, and then I started recruiting, and the next thing you knew the seniors started showing up.

I never ascertained whether Miguel was retired or not necessarily looking for employment, but he was not one to be rushed. When he spoke, it was only two or three decibels above a whisper, but he almost always cleared his throat to prepare you to listen. Miguel was my best student, and he could instantly switch roles and become my most competent aide-de-camp when the class accommodated a new student, or a student got hopelessly lost on the internet.

I would say, "Miguel, por fi, ayúdame con este nuevo estudiante," and that meant Miguel would prompt the new student to our home page, and orient them by, for example, placing the cursor in the field reserved for URLs, or by jumping from field to field stroking the Tab key. Miguel would make sure the students' screens were maximized and that the concept of "tabs" was firmly ensconced in their neophyte brains. This was a sight to behold, and I liked to ask Miguel to help me out a little more each class as a way of building his confidence and also as a way to differentiate the learning a little. The first ten minutes of class were devoted to teaching students not to peck at their keyboards like misanthropic pigeons, but to approach the keyboard and the monitor in front of them as a platform they could maneuver without their eyes; that is, with the same "blindness" they might use when changing the channel on a remote in a dusky room, or dialing a phone number without actually looking at the touchpad.

Most librarians shy away from working in the hood, that is, "librarianing" in working-class neighborhoods that have higher rates of petty theft and violent crime; some librarians might even believe that the ten or more classes they took in library school entitle them to not "see" poverty and engage with its many symptoms. Moreover, the level of entitlement in wealthier libraries is troubling when the need is so real in underserved libraries. After working at libraries in prosperous West LA, I don't know if I can honestly say that the libraries in South Central are more dangerous, or conversely, that police arrive with more alacrity in a wealthy neighborhood. I worked for about two years in a place where no one questioned my pedigree or my educational level, or if I went to a brick-and-mortar university or an online one, because I was there to help, and that's all that mattered.

In my book, "safe" libraries are mausoleums for James Patterson novels; a good library, by contrast, is messy, noisy, boisterous, and sometimes smells like free-lunch milk (especially if they're running a summer lunch program) and ossified sponges. If the books are grubby and the carpet is a little stained, then as far as I'm concerned, that is a library that is being used, and brothers and *hermanitas*, there is nothing more glorious than a humming library that is firing on all pistons, fulfilling holds, blurping barcodes, answering tutoring questions, and helping grandmas print out Bible verses, Facebook pics, or directions to the *Ellen DeGeneres Show*. The books almost walk themselves out of the library and onto the nightstands, nooks, and cubbies of readers when their activities, attitudes, and proclivities match what's going on inside the library. Thus, you can have a top-notch library in the middle of great need, and you can have a super mediocre library at a branch that's flush with dough.

As I've said, Miguel was a soft-spoken Latino man who I used to give computer lessons to as part of the weekly classes that I ran at the library. I say "was" because I don't work at *that* library anymore, but the poise I earned and the gratitude I learned while working with the adult students at the Vernon library are things that I won't easily forget. Miguel sticks out in my memory because of the guilt I felt on getting a promotion and having to move to a different region of LA. I don't work in South Los Angeles anymore, an area I had to commute to. Now I work in a region of LA where patrons will argue with you over a fifteen-cent fine. But there are deep pockets of need firmly ensconced in the genetic makeup of all our fancy zip codes, and rapidly gentrifying neighborhoods ensure that libraries remain integral community spaces, regardless of zip code, social stratum, or educational level.

I don't serve too many Miguels in my new capacity because my position, objective, and focus have all changed. When I was helping Miguel to figure out the difference between a URL and an e-mail, I was an adult librarian in South Central Los Angeles. Now I rove the libraries in my region trying to make connections between immigrant communities and their closest libraries. But I always come back to Miguel and his example and the somewhat pernicious idea that *abuelitos and abuelitas* might be the demographic most left behind by the ubiquity of computers and smartphones. Ponder their plight with me: their grandchildren, all of whom are "digital natives," refuse to translate, let alone contextualize, the digital reality they feel as real, let alone teach the grandparents how to negotiate an auto-form, or reveal the source code of a website, or explain the operating principle behind a meme.

You can only imagine what a great honor it was for me that a student would travel to get to my free computer library class, that is, invest their own gas money to get themselves to my class. Again, ponder with me the circuitous route that got Miguel to this point: an immigrant Latino senior citizen, far from home, suffering from exile erasure, but with enough chutzpah to seek out the brown library man leading a ragtag brigade of Spanish-speaking senior citizens, and warming up the projector, unscrolling the screen, and asking *estudiantes* to sign in.

Project Code

~ BRANDY MCNEIL ~

Coming from the private sector to libraries has been a disruptive change, but also an amazing journey for me. I am a true believer in customer service, and after coming from a company which had built its reputation and business on customer service, I was so happy to find that the library was a place where good customer service still holds strong and true—that it is, in fact, at the core of the mission. If you had asked me a few years ago, as I was pursuing my degree in entrepreneurship, if I had ever considered working in libraries, the answer would have been a resounding "no." Libraries were not even on my radar. Today, I can't imagine things any other way. I wake up every day loving every aspect of my job. I used to feel that maybe I was not doing enough to help other people and perhaps I needed to volunteer more. Now, I remind myself that what I do every day is helping people in profound ways, in ways I could not have imagined. My work is a privilege, and I can't imagine not doing what I am doing today, as part of the New York Public Library (NYPL), to help people learn and develop the skills that make them more confident and competent and make their lives better.

As the associate director of adult tech education for the New York Public Library, I have an incredible opportunity to help impact people's lives in both super-small and larger-than-life ways. At the beginning, my work was focused on tech training for staff in the branches throughout the library system. The training focused on the basics, ensuring that all staff have what they need to be successful in their jobs. Through this TechConnect work, I began to learn not only about the basic training needs of the system's huge staff, but also about the areas of skills development and tech learning that were ripe for possibility and potential. I was asking the questions: "What does the staff need to know about tech?" and "What types of training will be most helpful to them in their work?" Soon I became interested in asking those same questions about our branch patrons. "What do people need?" "What types of training will help them in their lives?"

I received a promotion that set the groundwork for me to begin to think about tech training for patrons. One of my first goals was to decentralize that training. I understood that the NYPL had built a culture around brand loyalty, and in order to bring new tech experiences to the library, the same patrons who know and trust the library brand needed to begin to see the library as a tech educator and leader. I needed to capitalize on that customer loyalty. As with all change, it was also important for me to be sensitive and aware of the staff's response to my vision to evolve the library's tech offerings. I made it a priority to meet with departments throughout the system on a monthly basis not only to share my goals and visions for TechConnect, but also to listen and learn about their concerns. It was very important to build those bridges to ensure that my colleagues and peers were on board with and felt a part of these new initiatives. It was also essential to begin to align the initiative's goals with the goals of the larger New York City community. For instance, the mayor of New York was talking to the media about his "Coding for All" campaign for New Yorkers. Suddenly, Coding Boot Camps began popping up all over the city. I saw clearly that the library could be the key in leveling the field for all people to have equal access to the opportunity to learn to write computer code. The Boot Camps were not free, and most of the camps were available only during the workday. Many of the people who would benefit most from access to these skill-building opportunities work during the day, have work or family commitments that limit their ability to attend a series of mandatory classes, or might not have the money to pay for this type of opportunity. It became a call to action for me and my staff to develop schedules for our classes that would allow working people to attend at least two classes a week and to make those classes available at no cost. In order to acquire the dollars that we needed to make this happen, it was necessary to concentrate our initial efforts on branding and marketing in order to get the message out to people across the city that these classes were available, and to partner with businesses and community leaders in order to gain support and resources for the project. It also became clear that we needed to reach out to the Boot Camps and develop a partnership with them; this would ensure the best possible learning outcomes for our patrons by arranging opportunities for graduates of Project Code to attend the Boot Camps to continue their learning and skill-building.

When I conceived of the Project Code program, I had no clue if what we were doing was going to work; maybe it would end up just being a little experiment. Nonetheless, true to my entrepreneurial mindset, I was more than ready to jump in and take the risk. I approached this project as a start-up. I strategically built my team, seeking out people who are excited about tech and interested in helping others. It was less important to me what degrees or experience my potential team members had; what was most important was to find people who have a passion for people and a passion for teaching. My team and I worked hard to prepare to launch our vision in 2013. We had worked diligently to come up with processes for the orientation and testing of new students, and to manage the program. What happened next defied all of our expectations.

I remember it like it was yesterday. We prepared the room to seat approximately thirty people and had our presentation slides ready to go. Before we could even get downstairs, I received a call from security asking, "Hey, what do you want us to do with this line of people?" Still thinking it was only a few people, I said, "Just line everyone up along the side."

By the time I got downstairs, the line was out the door and we had 300 people in that line along the side. Three hundred people had showed up wanting the opportunity to learn to code, at the library, at no cost to them.

To make sure that the program was meaningful for patrons and that they would feel like they were learning something tangible and transferrable, something practical, we reached out to partner with the NYPL's Business Library. The Business Library hosts a popular small-business competition each year. I thought that it would be ideal to partner with the participants in this competition by creating an opportunity for our Project Code students to build websites for these small businesses. The mutually beneficial results were amazing! The small businesses had the opportunity to see what it is like to work with a developer to create their brand and vision through a website, and our students had the opportunity to experience real-world applications of their hard work as they developed websites for the businesses.

To date, our program has seen over 6,000 people on a waiting list, and the seats in the program fill up in less than ten minutes each new semester.

However, in spite of these extraordinary numbers, it's what we have been able to help people accomplish that has been truly fulfilling for me. The letters I receive from patrons prove to me that the work we do in the library is truly a catalyst, a launching pad to success. One patron wrote us a letter and stated: "As you have all been a part of my journey from reluctant/insecure woman in tech to full stack developer, I'd like to let you know that in a week I begin the next part of my journey as a Front End Web Developer Intern at *NY Magazine!*" So many women of all ages and demographics have gained not only skills but also confidence through their participation with Project Code. In fact, 60 percent of the graduates of Project Code are women!

A woman who was part of one of the small business competitions was at the start of her career as a fashion designer. Our students created a website to help her develop her brand and raise her profile. This designer and her website eventually appeared in *British Vogue* magazine. In addition, she is now a Tory Burch Fellow.

Another Project Code patron who completed our Phase 1 and Phase 2 workshops ended up working for the organization in which we started our partnership with Codecademy. She became a teaching advisor for their Pro platform and now helps users who are stuck in HTML, CSS, and a few other computer languages.

A young fashion designer on the *Project Runway* show utilized our YouTube class, "How to Build Your Brand on YouTube," to help her develop and expand her brand.

One woman came to every class she possibly could. At the time, she did not have a job and she was really struggling hard to learn. But she kept on coming. When she was ready, my team prepared her for the interview of a lifetime. We were all so proud when she told us that she not only got the job, but she was so grateful for our help that she planned to donate her first paycheck to the library branch in which she had built her skills.

Another patron, who was in our Office Readiness series, was able to become a Microsoft Office Certified Specialist as a result of the courses she took at the Countee Cullen Library. It is amazing to help not just our patrons, but businesses in the community that need to upskill their staff as well. A great example is our partnership with the Bronx Botanical Gardens, where we enjoyed the opportunity to train their staff in Microsoft Excel.

These are just a few examples of the people that Project Code has touched, among the countless patrons who have gotten jobs, promotions, or passed certification exams as a result of their participation in Project Code.

But it's also the little things that play a huge role in people's lives. In my iPhone class for seniors, we have helped grandparents learn how to send emojis to their grandkids. The smiles, the excitement, and the joy we witness after their grandkids respond with praise are so gratifying. My experiences teaching tech at the New York Public Library have shown me how libraries are essential and what a difference they make in people's lives. We are what keeps some people from being left behind in the digital world, and we are an anchor for those who feel that, through the library, they can at least start to understand a world that is constantly changing before their eyes. Whether it's a patron who sends an e-mail thanking us for Mandarin Chinese computer classes when his area only offered Cantonese, a patron who is learning how to download podcasts to hear their preacher from church, or a student learning video-editing so they can create a documentary about their father, *it's the people working in the library who help to launch them into their next dimension, making us some of the most important people in our patrons' lives.*

A Love Letter to the Chattanooga Public Library

~ MEREDITH LEVINE ~

What Is Love?

In September 2015, I took a risk and moved to the South, to a place I was only familiar with because of a song that sang about a "Choo Choo." I left my family and all that I knew, and I hoped that this decision would lead me in the right direction. Life is about taking chances and finding love through new experiences, right? I never knew how much I could love a city, and the start of that love story was at 1001 Broad Street in downtown Chattanooga, Tennessee.

What is love, you may ask. A deep intense feeling for someone or something? The library became who I was in Chattanooga; maybe that isn't the healthiest thing in a "relationship," but it was all I could think about. "How can the Chattanooga Public Library *truly* become the catalyst for lifelong learning?" I jumped right in when I got there and was hired on as the head of youth services. I had a small staff, and soon I was able to add more, and I got to manage a project to build a state-of-the-art recording studio that came to fruition in the summer of 2017. In a bid to expand its reach, I took on the responsibility of managing the incredible makerspace on the 4th floor of the Downtown Library. I also started sitting on local boards and committees, and I was suddenly at the table helping to make decisions for the customers I was serving and create opportunities for the staff I was leading.

I was falling in love.

Things Were Getting Serious: More Than a Makerspace

You know when they say, "You are in love when you see that person every-where"? Walking through downtown Chattanooga, I begin to see our library's impact at every turn I take. From customers sitting waiting for the bus who will yell at me, "Hey, library lady," to someone from the mayor's office asking how our "Make. Play. Read. Learn." program is going this summer at an Innovation District Happy Hour event at the Edney building. But if I look even deeper than that, I start to see our library's impact on the windows, the telephone poles, and even on the backs of our citizens. When I walk by the Local Juicery on Main Street, I notice the vinyl lettering on their door letting everyone know they're open until 5:00 p.m. and it hits me: those numbers were made on the 4th floor. Late on a Friday night at the Bitter Alibi on Houston Street, I try to find the bathroom through a sea of people, and I notice that the "Restroom" sign too was made on the 4th floor. I want to grab a coffee on my way to a meeting at Mad Priest Coffee Roasters and see their logo of a stoic priest engraved onto a piece of wood, and I realize that that too was made on the 4th floor. On Instagram I watch a story from Scout, a local men's clothing store, and see that they are selling "Chatt Vibes" shirts, and I smile, knowing that those shirts were pressed in our makerspace. As I walk down the street, I wonder, *Who is C-Grimey?* I see those stickers on almost every electric pole and garbage can in downtown Chattanooga, and I realize that the hard-working rapper of that name made those stickers on the 4th floor (and he works there now, too).

These are just a handful of stories among many of local entrepreneurs, creatives, and everyday people who found themselves on the 4th floor and took advantage of the opportunity that was specifically designed for them. The 4th floor has leveraged itself as a mainstay in the community by creating a low entry barrier for any person who wants to make something.

The 4th floor is unique among library makerspaces due to its massive size (12,000 square feet) and dedicated staff, but what makes it even more unique is the customer's ability to just come in and make something on the spot. There are no waivers, no required trainings (except for equipment like the CNC router), and you can literally walk in, say you need to 3D print something, and we will assist you in your project. The staff are very clear that they will not make anything for you but give you the knowledge and tools you need to get started on your project. If a customer is struggling with a certain piece of equipment or software, we will let them know about our one-on-one appointments where they can get forty-five minutes of dedicated time to go more in-depth with their project. What we have found is that having the ability to walk in and walk out with something a patron has made in one visit is crucial for making everyone feel welcome and produces a natural creative energy.

I am not sure what I loved more, seeing the 4th floor out in the community or the community that was forming on the 4th floor. I would walk upstairs to check on the staff and see if they needed anything, and I would see how proud they were at the work the customers were doing themselves. Ellie Newell would be glowing while planning the next Weekend Craft Club program for our adult customers downstairs on the 1st floor, seeing the woman she helped with a sewing one-on-one the week before coming in to work on hemming her dress. Many times I would find Ellie and teen librarian Crissy Varnell getting excited about the upcoming months of Sew What that they were planning. And *shibori* dyeing on the front lawn of the library? Why not? This team was making the fiber arts available to everyone.

Cameron Williams (aka C-Grimey) would be caught high-fiving all the people he knew in town who were lining up to use the vinyl plotter, while he set them up on our music station to work on making a beat, and they would ask for Cam's opinion on the tracks they had just laid down. Cam's connections in the community and longtime use of the 4th floor as a customer gave us credibility. It is rare that you see patrons in their twenties or thirties spending several evenings a week at their local library, but this was happening on the 4th floor because of the people working in the space and the environment we had created, which made it inviting for everyone.

The best feeling was when the place was buzzing; someone was on the piano playing a song; kids were in the virtual reality booth; a new entrepreneur was designing her logo on Illustrator; Jaclyn Anderson, a head librarian on her lunch break, was coming up to work on her animations for the punk show at the Palace Theater; Michael Grilo was teaching a customer about the laser cutter; families were making buttons; and of course, something was always being printed on the 3D printer. And there was poor Michael, our only full-time employee on the 4th floor; all of that buzzing would usually be happening when he was the only person on the floor, but after the rush had tailed off, his passion for making in libraries would be validated time and time again. Michael's dedication to the space and its success was a motivator for me to continue to push the library leadership to support the maker efforts in the system. As much as it was stressful and tiring, these guys love what they do, and I loved watching them turn this space into what it is today. Making was not just for the "boys" anymore; the staff and the transformation of the space had truly made *making for all*.

Just like love takes work, so does creating a truly inclusive space. The 4th floor had to expand its hours, we had to get a programming budget, and we had to make sure that our wide array of customers had equitable access to the 4th floor. We were getting busier and busier on the 4th floor, and we needed more staff participation. I took a note from my previous job at the Fayetteville Free Library, where every professional librarian had to work a shift in the FabLab. Accordingly, teen and adult services staff started filling in shifts on the 4th floor, and we saw more staff and more customers starting to come up to the space.

The equipment in the makerspace can be intimidating, but it really is not that hard to use. When someone at the circulation desk can confidently talk to you about sewing or 3D printing, they're going to be that much more convincing to the customer they're talking to. Part of the work we had to do was to identify what our community needed. At our branch libraries, the customers really wanted 3D printers; we were pivoting from 3D printing downtown, but we supported our branches to get one. Our most-used piece of equipment is the vinyl plotter, and the staff put together a request to get a heat press, and that was a game changer. Once word got out that you could make your own shirts at the library, our reach spread like wildfire. We had families coming in making shirts for family reunions, high school kids coming in to work on their clothing line, and countless adult customers using the machine to further their brand. This equipment was literally putting the community's tax dollars to work and putting those dollars back in the community. It was beautiful. And then there were local creatives, like Steve Bedford's iTRAP brand; I'd see those shirts of his out in the community and in pictures surfacing on social media. I would get a message on Facebook from Heatherly, a local songwriter, who asked if we had the equipment at the library for her to press shirts before she went on tour, and the answer was "yes." One night we had a punk band come up just to use our tables to screen print their shirts before hitting the road. What we do in libraries is give people the information, the tools, and the space they need to better their lives and their minds, and we can do the same in our local economies as well.

Sometimes we even get something back. I saw a flyer for a benefit at the Palace Theater where a portion of the proceeds would be donated to the 4th-floor makerspace. I reached out to Amy Mayfield, previous owner of the local record spot, Mayfield's All Killer No Filler Records, and thanked her for thinking of us. The few hundred dollars she sent was so kind, but what was even kinder was Amy responding by asking if she could donate her old screen-printing press and conveyor-belt dryer to the library. Of course we said yes, and again we had the opportunity to up our game by giving our customers industry-standard equipment for them to learn and hone their skills on.

A former employee of the Chattanooga Public Library, Megan Emery, started the Creative Entrepreneurs Conference, where we invited local creatives to learn from each other and learn about the tools the library had for them to make their creative endeavors a reality; everything from marketing and branding, to legal advice, to how to exhibit at the Chattanooga Market. We are not only showcasing what the 4th floor has to offer but connecting people with each other to build a stronger creative community in our city. Megan's efforts with the online Etsy Community brought in some really valuable partnerships, like one with clothing designer Eileen Fisher. Her company gave the library boxes of clothes that had minor flaws so they couldn't be sold in stores, but we were able to upcycle the fabric into new items. At the 2017 Maker Faire, participants got to pick out an Eileen Fisher garment and upcycle it into an infinity scarf. Making at its best!

The Maker Faire was brought back to the library; we were able to exhibit fifty makers in 2018 and had thousands of people come through our doors for the experience. With these efforts, we were able to participate in the Nation of Makers Conference, which was hosted last year in Chattanooga. We have won our case that making is something that belongs in libraries and in the Chattanooga community, and I can't wait to see where the 4th floor goes next.

You begin to realize that the library is more than just a building filled with books. The library is Chattanooga, and Chattanooga is the library. I've always said that if you want to see how well your community is doing, spend an afternoon at the library. And as an employee, I can just sit back and watch the magic happen.

I fell in love.

Love Is in the Air Waves: The Studio at the Chattanooga Public Library

On your way home, you turn on 88.1 WUTC, Chattanooga's local NPR affiliate station, and you hear a melodic beat and catchy vocals; it sounds like the local band I Can Japan. You realize it is them, and then the soothing English voice of Richard Winham comes on and says you are listening to "Live in the Library," a thirty-minute set recorded live in the Studio at the Chattanooga Public Library.

When the Studio at the library opened in July 2017, I felt like my baby was going off to kindergarten; they were either going to flourish or suffer. I may sound like the overly proud parent who thinks her child is the smartest in the class, but my love for the Studio and what it has become is something I will be proud of forever. It was a labor of love.

The Studio was a big hit. The local newspaper, the Chamber of Commerce, the Mayor's Office, and more were coming in to use our space to record; we had everyone from the chief of police to Richard Lloyd from the band Television using the space. Chattanooga Girls Rock campers were coming in to make a podcast talking about the "hard issues" to our teenage boys' podcast, "K.I.1.: Keeping It 100." From customers who were already established musicians to others who just had an idea in their head and wanted to get it out, this space was now available to them all, and all they needed was a library card. Charles Allison, an expert in the field of audio recording, was our first full-time library employee to work in the Studio. He shared a story of a customer who showed up almost an hour late to Charles's three-hour Open Studio session and was drenched in sweat. He rapped with a towel over his head and he was good, real good. Charles said he sounded like André 3000 from OutKast. After the session, the customer apologized for being late and told Charles his alarm hadn't gone off, and when he woke up and realized he had his session, he ran three miles to get to his appointment at the library. Open Studio is a free service for our patrons; the customer could have just skipped the session at no cost to him, but he valued the time that was available to him to bring his music to life. This was a moment that has lasted with Charles forever. Music is something we all enjoy, and it shouldn't just be for the select few who have the means to make it.

One customer in particular who is a true library success story is Kevin. Kevin is visually impaired and has worked with the Hart Gallery in Chattanooga, where he has made paintings depicting Prince, Wednesday Addams, and others. Kevin wanted to record a song, "Pretty Eyes." A loop was found, and he sang his song; all of the lyrics were in his head. To this day, Kevin has made several songs about his fantasies, his life story, and more; he has a YouTube channel with his songs being played over a painting he made. He even got to perform "Pretty Eyes" out on the library's plaza on Make Music Day. Where else in a community could someone like Kevin walk in and leave with recorded songs that he wrote in his head?

This was real love.

Love Is in the Details: The 2nd Floor

On the 2nd floor, teen librarian Crissy Varnell saw art in what everyone else regarded as just leftovers. Vinyl scraps cut into circles line the concrete floor, paper globes float above the collection all made by teens, and colorful melted plastic bottles have been turned into a Chihuly-inspired sculpture. More vinyl scraps were used to create a DIY version of Yayoi Kusama's Obliteration Room, which allowed kids to experience fine art. Suddenly, the 2nd floor was not only getting its own look, but it was made by the kids who were there. Seeing your own efforts in the spaces you frequent is so empowering.

With the help of 2nd-floor staff, we made sure that the 4th floor was just as inviting for our youth as it was for our adults. Our Teen Tech programs and Zine Making programs were starting to gain popularity. We wanted to create a linear experience for library customers. We noticed that there could be a gap; after storytime, some kids never come back into the library, and after high school graduation, some students never come back until they became parents. So we purposely made an effort to make sure there is something for everyone at our library.

Thanks to a partnership with the University of Tennessee at Chattanooga, we received seven beautiful electronic pianos; two were placed on the 4th floor, one was put in the Studio, and four were out in the 2nd-floor teen center. We had easy-to-read sheet music placed out for any kid to take a seat and start playing piano. We saw kids teach themselves how to play, and even though we heard the theme song to *Halloween* over and over again, it was a beautiful sound to our ears when students were teaching themselves how to play an instrument that is the gateway to a musical universe. This access was the starting point to our small recording setup on the 4th floor, and then into an Open Studio session in the Studio.

The core staff made the 2nd floor into a reflection of the teens we had coming in every day. Some of these kids would arrive at 9:00 a.m. when we opened and leave at 8:00 p.m. when we closed. It was a tough job, but we were working to create lifelong library users. Teenagers are a very difficult age group to work with, and with our two departments we were able to see kids who aged out of the 2nd floor and then found their new home on the 4th floor. We created a space where a nineteen-year-old who had aged out of the 2nd floor could find a place that was just as cool and inspiring just two floors up!

This was true love.

Moving On

My four years at the Chattanooga Public Library felt like a lifetime. I felt I had known these people my whole adult life. I felt I knew the customers and the people running the city as if they were friends and family. They say you have three great loves in your life. The Chattanooga Public Library is one of mine. I went out to Los Angeles for a visit in April 2019 and had that feeling in my gut that this was where I needed to be. I needed to leave the Chattanooga Public Library, and I did so in August 2019. Now I have embarked on a new adventure with the LA County Library. I look from afar at the great work the team in Chattanooga is continuing to do, and I hope others can experience this kind of love for their library. Sometimes it requires stepping back and watching others as they maneuver through your space to see how magical the field we are in truly is.

Anonymous Man

~ SUE CONSIDINE ~

There is a quote that I keep in my "how to better understand people and the world toolkit" that we are all probably familiar with: "Be kind, for everyone you meet is fighting a battle you know nothing about." This simple maxim calls to mind all of the ways that libraries support people as they move through their own unique life journeys and pursue their aspirations and dreams. As I think about and reflect on this, I am reminded of the basic truth for all of us who live and breathe Library; we are essential; we support, elevate, transform, and save lives; we connect people; and we make the world a better place for everyone. Attendance and circulation numbers, successful programs and events, door counts . . . these are all data that help us understand, in a quantitative way, how library expenditures support the library participation of individuals in the community. These data are a useful tool because they inform us as we redefine and design our spaces, services, and access. But this data does not tell the story—our stories—of impact, learning, discovery, value, and the true meaning of the library in the lives of the community.

My story is the result of a surprise visit from Jane, the out-of-town daughter of Anonymous Man. For years, an Anonymous Man came to the library on a regular basis, headed to the fireplace sitting area, grabbed a newspaper, and spent the day reading and snoozing in a comfortable chair located near the Café. The Café is a place of activity and is typically buzzing with conversation, games, and connection. In this vibrant space, you will find children playing together at a train table with puzzles and games. While parents catch up and connect with each other after a storytime, students of all ages fill the Café and adjacent reading room, teachers grade papers and sip coffee, and tutors work with students to support their learning. By contrast, Anonymous Man never checked out a book, chatted with staff at the circulation desk, attended a program, or sipped a cup of coffee in the Café. He was content to sit in his chair and just *be* in the library near the Café, where the people gather.

One day, I had a visit from a woman I had not met before in my office. Jane—I have changed her name—had a story to tell. She shared an obituary with me and to my surprise, it was that of Anonymous Man, a man who had never participated actively in the library, never asked a thing of us, never made himself known in any way. We have all been in the position, during a busy day, when we are faced with an unexpected, unscheduled visit from a member of the public. Often, the purpose of the visit is to share an idea or concern, and we take the time to listen and promise to consider the issue as we hurry back to the pressing priorities of the day. I immediately understood that this woman's visit was different, and I switched gears to focus on her and clear my schedule for the afternoon in order to give her my full attention. Jane began by sharing with me that her father had visited the library every week to read the paper and just get out of his house to be "where the people are." She explained that he was an introvert and could appear to be unfriendly because he didn't wish to draw attention to himself. Continuing, Jane shared how he would talk to her about "his library," "his chair," the nice people who were like "family" to him that work there, and how he enjoyed seeing the children playing and having fun. It was clear to her that he felt the library was like home and was a place where he could experience the simple pleasure of belonging and being in close proximity to other people.

We settled in to talk, and I realized that it was very important to Jane that I understand who her father was, beyond the quiet man who sat in a chair in the library. Anonymous Man had always been humble and reclusive. Jane explained how, growing up, her father had been her ally and confidant. She could tell him anything, and he made her feel safe and accepted. As a private man, he didn't have much of a social life and spent most of his time at home, engaged in solitary activities. He spent his days in retirement with crosswords and Sudoku. He was whip-smart and enjoyed watching and playing *Jeopardy* on TV. He developed a carefully curated library in his home; his diverse reading interests included everything from military history to cooking and canning. With pride and admiration, Jane shared how he loved and cherished his wife and daughter and was always a gentleman. He referred to his wife as his bride and never failed to open doors for women. After serving in the military, he spent his work life with the same company, where he was well-liked and was regarded as a good employee and a good man, with a sly and dry sense of humor. Jane talked about his face, describing how on the outside he might appear closed, tired, and unapproachable, but his eyes, which were deep brown and expressive, were the true windows on his real personality. His eyes, like his humor, were bright and expressive. She said that his weekly routine included a trip to the bakery, to the cemetery to visit his wife, and to the library.

Jane explained that she is much like her father, and is most happy and comfortable at home, surrounded by familiar things like her books and pets. We talked about how the library had been a passive yet crucial piece of her father's happiness in his later years, and she thought that she might look for ways to utilize a library herself back home, as she was now nearing retirement. I silently wished that she might join a book club or attend a lecture series or consider learning how to sew. As her father recognized that he could find a sense of community and closeness to other people through his regular visits to the library, my hope was that Jane too could find that sense of belonging. I also understood that this was not the time to share a laundry list of engagement opportunities that a library might provide for her; this was her time to honor and remember her father and share his story. I felt intensely proud that Jane, as a private person herself, chose to share details of herself and her father's story with me.

That afternoon was a true Eureka moment for me; I was affected in a profound way, connecting directly with my heart to both Anonymous Man and his proud daughter. That afternoon resonated with me, but it also rattled and shook me to my librarian core: what an enormous responsibility we have; what we do every day really matters; oh no, what if I am not doing enough; what if what I am doing is not the right thing; could I have done more, and if so, what? Strangely enough, this beautiful story, shared by his daughter, made me feel inadequate and frightened. I worried that there is so much more to do, and am I, are we, are our libraries doing all we can to support people like Anonymous Man? This visit reinvigorated my commitment, as a public library administrator, to continuously seek out ways to leverage our resources and facilities to meet the less obvious, but equally critical, needs of all the people we have the honor to serve. It also underscored the clear and crucial need for physical public library spaces in every community, even in this rapidly evolving digital age. Every community has an Anonymous Man/Woman/Teen/Child, and their needs matter.

Let's take a moment and imagine all the people, of all ages, on the fringes of our communities and right in front of us, who will never tell us what the library means to them, but are in our libraries on a daily basis. When we hear decision-makers and stakeholders talk about how there is a lack of value in investing in physical libraries in the digital age, remember Jane and Anonymous Man's story and add yours—you know you have one, at least one. Imagine a community without the library, the space that provides a connection to a common humanity for so many who are alone, lonely, and otherwise on the fringes. Imagine a world without the librarians and library workers who provide access to the spaces, content, technologies, tools, and resources that elevate the lives of the individual and the community, that make the people on the fringes feel as though they are family, that they belong, that they matter, like Anonymous Man. The answer, sometimes, is as simple as a comfortable, thoughtfully placed chair in close proximity to "where the people are."

Anonymous Man reminds us of our purpose and power as librarians and library workers. You are an equalizer. You do magical, essential, critical work that takes all your resources, time, energy, emotions, empathy, talent, intellect, and most importantly, your heart. You are more than likely underpaid, overworked, and pulled in too many directions for any human being to bear every single day. Yet you remain, as do libraries, as that unique, irreplaceable force of good in our communities, making lives better, every day.

Flux Capacitor

~ JOHN SPEARS ~

"This is the best library in the world!" Those words echoed through the cavernous Knights of Columbus Hall, a building that is part of the Penrose Campus of the Pikes Peak Library District, near midnight on Saturday, June 24, 2017. They were not shouted by a teen discovering a makerspace for the first time, an adult attending a reading by one of her favorite authors, or a child enthralled by a performer. Instead, these words were bellowed to a group of fans by a member of a punk rock band between songs at the first concert to be held at that location in over eighty years. How four punk rock bands—Autumn Creatures, Turvy Organ, Blind the Thief, and Curta—found themselves performing in an inaugural concert at a library involves the unlikely intersection of a ninety-year-old building that had undergone numerous transformations over the years, a tragic and fatal warehouse fire in Oakland, and a determined artist collective known as Flux Capacitor that refused to give up on their mission of bringing the DIY (Do It Yourself) and DIT (Do It Together) cultures to the residents of Colorado Springs, the second-largest city in Colorado.

The Knights of Columbus Hall had an inauspicious beginning, but it was a beginning that would find a strange symmetry in what it was to eventually become. As part of the world's largest Catholic service organization, the Colorado Springs Knights of Columbus Council 582 had existed in the community for years, providing aid and assistance to both native and immigrant Catholic communities, war and disaster relief, and a place for social gatherings. Lacking a building of their own, Council 582 began fundraising in 1924, and by 1928, they had raised enough money to enter into a contract with the famed local architect Thomas McLaren to design a meeting hall and community center, projected to cost $30,000. Dedicated on October 12, 1928, Knights of Columbus Hall was far from an uncontroversial building. Anti-Catholic bigotry was common at the time, and the mayor of Colorado Springs was publicly lambasted for speaking at the building's dedication. Despite the charitable aspirations of the Knights of Columbus, their actions were viewed with suspicion, and the Hall was seen as a home for those on the fringes of society. Although the Hall was offered as a space for public enjoyment, lectures, and communal gatherings, hostility toward Catholics was strong, and Council 582 found itself unable to maintain support for the building. By 1937, the situation had reached an untenable stage, and the Knights of Columbus were forced to sell their beloved Hall, which was meant to be a gathering place for all the residents of Colorado Springs regardless of their beliefs, to the city of Colorado Springs for $13,000.

Having purchased the building under somewhat questionable circumstances (and for a fraction of what it was worth), the city quickly transformed the Hall into the home of the Colorado Springs Pioneers Museum. As the Pioneers Museum, the Hall housed a collection of artifacts and memorabilia that had been recently donated to the city by the Colorado Springs Pioneer Association. The museum was a popular destination for those interested in the early days of Colorado history, and as more and more items were added to the collection, the museum eventually outgrew the Hall, leading to the construction of a 4,800-square-foot addition—the first of several projects that would radically transform the building. As a free museum, Knights of Columbus Hall was able to maintain its status as a public building for the next forty years. Originally built as a place for social gatherings, education, and community celebrations and then reborn as a public museum, its next iteration took the building out of the public sphere—a situation that would not be remedied until another forty years had passed.

By 1977, the building was proving to be woefully inadequate to showcase the museum's extensive collection, and finding itself in need of a larger space, the Pioneers Museum moved into the recently vacated El Paso County Court-house. Muir & Associates Architects took ownership of the Hall the following year and operated out of the facility until 1988. The firm's architects worked at desks in what had been the large assembly room during the Knights of Columbus period and the main gallery during the Pioneers Museum period. The firm built a catwalk over the floor of this large space to enable manage-ment to monitor the architects' work. Gone was the central meeting hall, capable of holding hundreds of people for dances, concerts, and events, and with each new construction project and each new owner, Knights of Columbus Hall drifted further and further from public use.

Following the departure of Muir & Associates, the building sat empty for three years until it was purchased by the Pikes Peak Library District in 1991 for $175,000. Situated next to the downtown Penrose Library, the Hall pro-vided a quick expansion for the landlocked library and was used for storage before eventually becoming the home for Technical Services, the Pikes Peak Library District Foundation, the Friends of the Pikes Peak Library District, overflow from the Regional History and Genealogy collection, and a series of assorted departments, including Facilities and Adult Education. Over the course of the next twenty-five years, the Pikes Peak Library District built new and larger buildings far from downtown, departments moved out, and the Hall gradually emptied, leaving only the Adult Education Department. The library district never forgot the original purpose of the building, though, and while it never seemed feasible to staff such a large facility, the hope was always there that one day the building could become a community space once again.

Years later and 1,200 miles away, on the night of December 2, 2016, disas-ter struck another building, one that had taken the opposite trajectory of Knights of Columbus Hall. Ghost Ship, in Oakland, California, was originally built as a warehouse but had become, like many warehouse spaces through-out the country, the home of an artist collective and included living spaces, galleries, and a concert venue. Near midnight, as artists from the 100% Silk record label were performing for a small audience, a fire broke out on the first floor and quickly spread through the lower level of the building, unbeknownst to those on the floors above. The building lacked sprinklers and smoke detectors, the hallways and spaces were filled with furniture and art, and the only staircases in the building—one of them built from wooden pallets—were hidden in the maze-like structure and did not lead directly to exits. Thirty-six people perished that night, the deadliest building fire in

California since the 1906 San Francisco earthquake. The fire, though, had ramifications far beyond Oakland, and many artist collectives throughout the United States suddenly found themselves under intense scrutiny and pressure to move from spaces they had used for years, lest another tragedy like Ghost Ship unfold. Colorado had long been a home for artists and musicians, but a crackdown on collectives inhabiting buildings deemed unsafe by the authorities quickly ensued. In the months that followed, three Colorado collectives were forced to shut down: Rhinoceropolis and Glob in Denver, and only three weeks after the warehouse fire in Oakland, Flux Capacitor in Colorado Springs.

The news of Flux Capacitor's closure was devastating to the arts community and local music scene in Colorado Springs. The collective had been formed just two years earlier in 2014 by Bryan and Sean Ostrow, two brothers with a nearly ten-year history of planning house shows, booking touring musicians, and performing in their own metal bands. Flux had recently celebrated the anniversary of its formation with a "Two Year Fluxiversary" concert. Operating out of a small warehouse space with an all-volunteer crew, the concert drew an eclectic mix of punk, metal, and indie rock bands, rappers, comedians, and spoken word, performance, and visual artists to an all-ages venue that welcomed everyone. As the foremost space for the DIY community in the region, Flux Capacitor hosted anyone with the desire and wherewithal to put on a show for their supporters. The closure of their venue, though, did not dampen their drive, and their loyal base quickly rallied to find a way—any way—for their shows to continue.

What followed was a town hall meeting on March 2, 2017, to look for another venue. Hosted by Kate Perdoni, a frequent performer at Flux with the band Eros and Eschaton, and Brian Elyo, who appeared as Mobdividual at Flux events, this town hall drew hundreds of people who had experienced Flux events in the past and longed to see them continue. Kate also happened to have worked at the Pikes Peak Library District in the past as an audio engineer at one of our recording studios, and she invited me to attend the event in my capacity as executive director of the library district. Not knowing much about Flux, the underground arts scene in Colorado Springs, or the DIY community outside of what I had witnessed in our own makerspaces, I was not sure what to expect. I can't help thinking, though, that Kate had a realization that she hoped I would arrive at on my own—the realization that Flux embodied everything a contemporary library strives to be: a gathering place, a space for creation, and a venue for those who lack a space of their own to share their talents, tell their stories, and have their voices heard.

At the town hall meeting, members of the DIY community, artists, and patrons of both passionately discussed what Flux had meant to them and the need to make sure it continued. Young adults described their first encounter with Flux and how they had finally found a place of like-minded individuals, free from judgment and accepting of them for who they were. Grandparents told of how Flux had created one of the few places in Colorado Springs where they could share in the excitement of a live performance with their grand-children. Members of marginalized communities praised Flux for welcoming them. Recovering addicts struggling to find a safe space to socialize talked about Flux as the only place in town where they could enjoy a punk, metal, or indie concert experience outside of a bar. Artists and musicians of all types held up Flux as the venue that was the first to provide them with a space to exhibit and perform, instilling in them a level of confidence that eventually allowed them to emerge on the broader arts scene. While every story was different, the message of everyone who spoke that night was united around one belief—the belief that Flux provided much more than just a space for concerts, performances, and art shows. Flux provided a sense of community to those who often felt they were on the fringes of society.

On its most basic level, Flux Capacitor was a core of volunteers dedi-cated to providing an outlet for the community to share their talents, come together, and celebrate their art, music, and performances. All they lacked was a building. Meanwhile, the Pikes Peak Library District, like many librar-ies, was struggling to connect with young adults in a meaningful way that would make them feel a part of the library. What we did have, though, was a building. Before the night was over, I texted Kate: "Are you free on Monday? Let's talk. I think I might have an answer for Flux."

What followed was a whirlwind . . . First came the task of convincing the library district's leadership team that we should consider partnering with an artist collective that had recently been kicked out of their home for code violations and was known for punk rock, metal, and provocative art shows. The fact that this partnership would involve the operation of a hallowed building with a nearly century-long history in the community gave me a certain amount of trepidation in making the proposal to them. Next would be convincing the board of trustees that this was an appropriate use for a building that had been seen for years as a natural expansion point for traditional library services, as the home of another makerspace and computer lab, and as meeting rooms. In a short period of time, our plans had changed from offering a place for programming *for* the community to offering a place for programming *by* the community. The passion of those involved with Flux, their descriptions of the possibilities they saw in that space, and the sudden groundswell of support for their cause were all that was required to convince both the leadership team and the board.

While Bryan and Sean were the heart and soul of Flux, they were quick to enlist several other artists and organizations in their quest to make Knights of Columbus Hall their home. Rebranding themselves as Flux 2.0, they brought to the board of trustees a roster of innovative artists and a slew of community-building proposals for how the space could be used in addition to the concerts they would hold. Jasmine Dillavou and JD Sell, graduates of the University of Colorado at Colorado Springs visual arts program, proposed the Non Book Club Book Club, an informal gathering that would bring together artists and the community in a shared discussion, free from what they called the "hierarchies" of the arts. Han Sayles and Peyton Kay Davis, printers with Peach Press, proposed zine and printmaking workshops for the public. Bread! COS, a "meal to micro-grant program for artists" run by Han and Mia Alvarado, sought to bring together local artists who were seeking funding with members of the community who were willing to pay ten dollars for a meal of soup and bread. During the meal, the artists would pitch their projects and the diners would vote on the most intriguing idea, with the winner receiving the money raised. These advocates' enthusiasm and innate understanding of what a public library can and should be overcame any hesitation that might have been felt, and the partnership of Flux 2.0 and the Pikes Peak Library District quickly became a reality.

Now, two years later, the partnership remains strong. Knights of Columbus Hall has hosted all of the events initially proposed to the board: bands from as far away as Venezuela and Germany have come to perform; a venue that allows both an experimental autoharpist and death metal bands to perform on the same stage at the same concert has been re-created; intergenerational poetry slams and workshops lasting well into the night are a monthly occurrence; and artists have shared pieces and installations that have explored everything from the experience of Puerto Ricans living on the U.S. mainland to the sexual mores and foibles of contemporary culture. Above all, though, the coming together of Flux 2.0 and the Pikes Peak Library District at Knights of Columbus Hall has succeeded in fulfilling the purpose for the building first laid out by Council 582 nearly a century ago. While it may seem strange to compare the members of a fraternal organization affiliated with the Catholic Church from nearly a century ago with a contemporary artist collective, in this instance, they are strikingly similar. Both have existed on the fringes of society, and both have a strong desire to give back to the community. The concert on June 24, 2017, was the first realization of that similarity, and although Bryan and Sean never suspected that Flux Capacitor would be reborn as Flux 2.0 with the assistance of their local library, what began on that night will ensure that the underground, DIY, and DIT art communities and the memory of the Knights of Columbus will continue to carry on in Colorado Springs.

Once Upon a Story

~ ERICA FREUDENBERGER ~

O nce upon a time, in a not-so-distant land where the river turned and the mountains rose, there lived a little library. A bit misshapen with barely a penny to its name, the library set out into the wide world, eager for adventure, curious about its neighbors, and ready to change the world. What was it thinking?

Sccccrrraaaaaatch (the sound of a needle pulled across a record). Let's try this again, shall we?

This story isn't a fairy tale. There are no heroes, princesses, witches, or dragons in it. There are no Herculean feats of strength, cunning plots, or hungry trolls salivating for a goat. There is, however, a small library determined to change the world—or at least its little village.

While this story isn't a fairy tale, it does contain powerful magic. It's about what happens when a community tells one story for so long that it forgets others. It's about weaving a new tale, dancing a new rhythm, and savoring a new delicacy. It's a cautionary tale with a quest involving strangers, riddles to unravel, and treasure to find.

It begins, as all great stories do, with the loss of something precious.

The Red Hook Public Library in New York's Hudson Valley is chartered to serve 1,961 people—the residents of the village of Red Hook. In practice, it serves nearly 10,000 people—all the residents of the town of Red Hook, along with the neighboring town of Milan. The people, for the most part, are happy. Red Hook is home to Bard College, some small family farms, and several historical sites. It's picturesque year round, whether dripping with lush greenery in the summer, dazzling with riots of orange, yellow, and red leaves in the fall, providing a spare, elegant beauty in the winter when trees become silver with ice and snow, or when gentle buds begin breaking out in the spring.

Human beings have called the Red Hook area home since at least 5,000 BC. It was part of Mohican territory inhabited by the Esopus and Sepasco tribes until Colonel Pieter Schuyler arrived in 1688, bringing Dutch surnames and traditions that remain, most notably in the Sinterklaas parade in neighboring Rhinebeck. The Palatines, German immigrants sent by the English to the Hudson Valley, arrived in the early eighteenth century, searching for a new home. The arrival of these immigrants began a demographic shift that remains centuries later—the population of Red Hook in the last census was 87 percent white. Traditions are deeply rooted too, as seen in the continued meeting of the Red Hook Society for the Apprehension and Detention of Horse Thieves, founded in 1796.

Although its mountain views, historic estates, and pastoral beauty continued to draw new residents to the region, the community's story, like the community itself, had not significantly changed, but it had taken on tones of conflict as new residents arrived. Concern about the influx of second-home owners, Bard College students, and more diverse new homeowners attracted by its school district caused rifts in the community. Old-timers feared the loss of family as the town's proximity to New York City caused local housing prices to escalate without an economic base to provide jobs, making home ownership untenable for their children. Newcomers were kept at arm's length and didn't understand many of the decisions—including the voting down of a sewer that would have allowed for economic development—being made by those who held elected office. Conflicts between the two groups flared up over the town's priorities, and the divide between old and new began to deepen.

The library, centrally located in the village, was housed in a mid-nineteenth-century building that had once been the home of a local tobacco baron.

Its octagonal shape reflected the influence of Orson Fowler, a nineteenth-century figure who dabbled in phrenology and architecture, and championed women's rights. The library had employed a part-time director and staff since its creation in 1898. In 2010, though, it welcomed its first full-time director (me), a stranger with vision, energy, and a profound belief in the power of community-led change. I assembled a plucky crew of nurses, scientists, students, artists, and musicians to set a new course for the library, and decided to invite all of Red Hook to bring their talents, creativity, and expertise to create a "stone soup" that would bring people together and nourish the community.

This marked a sea change in the direction and outlook of the library, which for many years had been off the radar of most residents, as tales of its being a forbidding and unfriendly place had spread from neighbor to neighbor. The first challenge my intrepid team and I faced was changing the image of the library by presenting it as an inviting space for all to create, learn, and grow. We knew we had a long, potentially perilous road ahead of us, but where to begin?

A trip to the chamber of commerce revealed the key. Make a Journey to Red Hook Together, a group of various stakeholder agencies that met every six weeks to discuss projects, had as its primary goal providing opportunities for cross-pollination and collaboration in the community. As we at the library managed to forge new relationships and court new partners, we soon found ourselves able to do much more than we had previously imagined. And as our capacity grew, so did our dreams.

In 2014, when ALA put out a call for libraries to take part in its Libraries Transforming Communities initiative, we scrambled to put together a band of five people, including Red Hook's deputy mayor, the director of Bard College's Center for Civic Engagement, and others. While we knew the odds of being chosen were not in our favor—ten teams would be chosen nationwide—we applied because we believed in the power of libraries to effect change, and we were committed to deeply engaging our community. We were shocked and delighted when we were chosen to participate. Our team members, who had volunteered, were stunned because we'd all believed that our chances were slim. This opportunity launched a quest, deep into the heart of the community, which changed our town and everyone who participated.

We received rigorous training in how to engage our community. The process began with a conversation—asking local people about their aspirations for the community and how they wanted to shape its future. The quest to solve the riddle of what mattered to people began by our going door-to-door, assembling groups of people at local businesses, and chatting with friends and neighbors at community celebrations. These conversations revealed a sense of longing. Although the community had long fought to remain homogeneous, it now wanted to embrace and celebrate diversity.

People told us they wanted to tell a story with more diverse voices, so we considered how the library could help. Our first opportunity presented itself as the nights grew longer, drawing a shadowy blanket over the town by 4:30 each evening. To ward off the darkness, friends and neighbors came together for one weekend each year for a Holiday in the Village. The celebration was nondenominational but involved lighting a large tree and an oversized menorah. Participants enjoyed hot cider and apple cider doughnuts at the Elmendorph Inn, where we celebrated Dutch Christmas. The story we told, as a community, was that this celebration represented our holidays, our community, and ourselves.

The Red Hook Public Library had a robust, ongoing collaboration with Bard College, and we had worked closely with a group of international students. As the years passed and our relationships deepened, these students became a part of our lives. Many were far from home and their families, and due to the great cost and distance of returning home, they would often not see their families for several years at a time. We were particularly close with some Indian, Nepali, Bangladeshi, and Sri Lankan students. They had led coding programs, Bollywood dance parties, and henna tattoo sessions at the library. They were a part of our library family, drawn to us, in part, because one of our library team was from Gujarat, India. We also knew that there were other South Asian families in town, so we decided to put together a Diwali celebration to complement the other holiday traditions in town.

Diwali is the Hindu festival of lights, celebrating the final harvest in late November or early December (depending on how the Hindu and Gregorian calendars align). Although it is traditionally a Hindu holiday, like Christmas in the United States, Diwali is embraced by other religions in India for its narrative: a celebration of the triumph of good over evil and knowledge over ignorance—a perfect message for the library to spread. During Diwali, people renew relationships and strengthen social bonds by lighting *diyas* (oil lamps), eating fried foods, setting off fireworks, and indulging in lots and lots of sweets—all the makings for a festive party!

As we began to plan for our first Diwali, we relied on the expertise of our friends and neighbors who had celebrated that festival for years. They, in turn, recruited others to help out, and we expanded our group to include a range of residents we hadn't yet met—doctors, pharmacists, artists, and others—who were eager to help make the project a success.

When the night of our Diwali celebration arrived, the white basement walls of the Masonic Temple drifted away, offering a glimpse into the lives and homes of our hosts. The fluorescent lights made the jewel-toned saris shine more brightly, and Priya's* dance costume—including intricate gold jewelry on her ankles, wrists, and head—shone like the sun as she demonstrated traditional dance moves. Farmers, hunters in camouflage, seniors, families, babies, and toddlers all were taken in by the swirling colors, the sands of the Rangoli, the lights of the *diya*, and the scents of Indian delicacies—*jalebi*, *gulab jamen*, and *chaat*. Dev and Rohan—a doctor and a pharmacist—had volunteered to staff the kitchen and were pleasantly surprised when they could barely keep up with the demand for the thick, orange mango juice that people were drinking by the gallon.

Stations were set up around the room for people to make *diyas*, the traditional Diwali lamps, play Parcheesi and *mancala*, learn to tie a sari, create intricate henna tattoos, and learn how and when to use cobra or deer hands while dancing. Indian music, children's laughter, and the gentle tinkling of hundreds of bracelets on attendees' arms filled the air.

Priya's grandmother, Amita, had arrived from India earlier in the day. After a grueling flight and a dramatic change in temperature, she was bundled up in a large down coat, with her back to the wall. She looked exhausted and overwhelmed but proud of her granddaughter's performance. Despite her travails, she volunteered to serve at the game station, where she oversaw the Parcheesi and *mancala* games. As the night wore on, her coat came off, and a smile spread across her face. By the end of the evening, she was challenging all comers to a game of *mancala*—she had serious skills—and was up for playing endless games with dozens of children. Her delight was infectious, and before the evening was over, she had promised to send Priya the family *mancala* board from India when she returned.

The faces of the international Bard students shone brightly: although they were far away from their own families, they had an ersatz extended clan who welcomed them—and all of us—into their home. They had a chance to celebrate their holiday with people who spoke their language, shared their customs, and understood their longing for connection. The students took turns helping at the henna tattoo, Rangoli, sari-tying, and *diya* stations—and

*All names in this story have been changed.

stuffed as much of the *jalebi* and other sweets as they could into their mouths (and at the end of the night, their purses and backpacks), eager for the familiar taste. At the end of the evening, Leela, an artist married to one of the doctors on mango juice duty, who had tied dozens of saris that evening, pulled me aside. "I've lived in Red Hook for forty years," she said. "This was the first time I ever felt I belonged."

Leela's words rocked me to my core. I thought about my arrival in the Hudson Valley more than a decade ago, and how alone I had felt in the beginning, but how I had gradually found my people and built my life. My path was easier than Leela's—most of the people around me looked like me and shared a similar culture and narrative. What would it be like to live somewhere for more than half your life and feel as if you didn't belong? What if there was no room in the community for your story?

By holding a Diwali celebration, we began to make a change in our community's narrative. Now, when people thought about Holiday in the Village, they still thought of carolers, of going to local businesses for cider and doughnuts, and Old Dutch Christmas at the Elmendorph Inn. They still looked forward to the lighting of a giant evergreen tree and a menorah. But they also thought of Diwali, of a riot of colors, smells, and tastes, of games and traditions that were less foreign with each passing year.

Our second Diwali celebration was hotly anticipated. Word had spread, and we had an even larger crowd (the first year had more than 170 people, while the second was well over 200). We moved to the firehouse so there would be room for everyone. Leela took charge of organizing the event, and we provided support. She pulled in more volunteers from the Indian/ Nepali/Sri Lankan community and had even more ideas for activities. When people arrived, they greeted each other affectionately—they had met a year ago, and now spoke when they saw each other around town. Everyone was excited. Many attendees dressed up in bright colors, excited to celebrate the occasion and take part in the festivities. Hugs and smiles passed easily. A week before the celebration, Anandhi came to my office at the library with a check for $500. She and her husband were committing to an annual donation so that the Diwali celebration could continue. (To put this in perspective, the library's budget line for adult programming for the entire year was less than $10.) The Singhs were donating money because the library had amplified their stories and traditions.

We didn't know when we began our Diwali journey where it would end. We knew it was an opportunity to amplify and treasure the voices and stories of our friends and neighbors. It also created experiences, memories, and relationships that propelled us through a dark winter, and began a larger conversation about who else needed to be at the table. We not only had a marvelous event but also strengthened the social fabric, unleashing talents and expertise that had been waiting in the wings. The Diwali event led to numerous other collaborations and community-wide celebrations where we learned to tango, make steamed dumplings, and make *arepas*.

Our experience with Diwali and subsequent celebrations underscored the importance of story in shaping the community. When we tell a story with limitations, we don't just exclude others; we stymie our growth and development. Expanding our stories enriches our lives and expands our horizons—and possibilities. It helps us to understand our place in an infinitely complex universe where each of us, as Walt Whitman says, contains multitudes. We are the stories we tell—our stories shape our world and determine our reality. Our narratives must have as much depth and be as rich and varied as all the members of our community. Our experience with Diwali reinforced the idea that public librarians aren't in the book business; we're in the story business—and it's our job to ensure that our narratives are as deep and wide as the people we serve.

Ben's Game

~ NICOLE GOFF ~

Does anyone really know what she wants to be when she grows up? I know a lot of answers to that childhood question are "reach-for-the-stars" type occupations: astronaut, ballerina, professional athlete, fairy godmother, cat. That last one was mine. I'm still waiting.

In the meantime, I've spent the past eleven years playing pretend at librarianship and have had the greatest surprise in that I really, really, *really* enjoy what I do. Don't get me wrong: it's not always rainbows and unicorn sprinkles. But there have definitely been more ups than downs, and it's all because of the people whom I've been blessed to serve.

I started my career in the public library system as a young adult librarian. I chose librarianship because (a) I'm an art history undergrad, and (b) I love to read. Books, not people, held my heart. And yet, as it turns out, librarianship is not about hoarding books like a dragon on a pile of gold. I have to admit, I was shocked when I realized that I was responsible for interacting with humans on a daily basis. And not just during my two to three hours on the reference desk. Programming? I was responsible for *getting people to come to the library?!* Outreach . . . (shudder). Networking . . . (hiss). Community engagement . . . (assume fetal position and wait for it to all be over).

But I liked it. My safety net of bookshelves became a social stomping ground where I got to share stories, lead arts and crafts, create a beautiful space for my teens, and connect with people. And though I now work in a school setting, I know my time as a public librarian gave me some of the best training for patron engagement.

As a public library, we saw regulars and new folks every day, as well as weekly group visits from nearby schools and other organizations. There was one group in particular that visited us about once every month, and they were some of my personal favorites. The group was comprised of about fifteen intellectually disabled adults and young adults who came to browse and borrow. A chaperone would usually accompany those individuals with specific needs, but for the most part everyone did his or her own thing. They'd peruse the shelves, read magazines, occasionally use our computers, and check out at the circulation desk when their visit was over.

From my spot at the reference desk, my interaction with this group was a bit limited. In fact, if I wasn't scheduled at the desk, chances are I might not see them at all for a couple months or more. Our library was two stories, and the upstairs was where the librarians' workspaces were located. Downstairs in the library proper, the circulation desk was the first thing people saw upon entering, with the reference desk positioned off to the left, adjacent to the adult fiction and nonfiction sections. The "fun stuff"—children's and young adult materials—was to the right of the circulation desk, and that's where this crowd usually spent their time. There was one young man, however, who would take the time to greet all of us at both desks when he came in and tell us all goodbye when he left. This was Ben.

When I remember repeat patrons, my memories of Ben are some of the most rewarding ones. I find myself smiling even now as I hear his voice in my head, "Hi, Librarian." He would ask our names every time he visited, but we were all "Librarian" in the end. A typical conversation might go something like this:

> **Ben:** Hi, Librarian.
> **Anne:** Hello, Ben.
> **Ben:** What's your name?
> **Anne:** My name is Anne.
> **Ben:** Hi, Anne.
> **Anne:** Hi, Ben.

> **Ben:** Okay, see ya.
> **Anne:** Bye, Ben.
> *Ben turns to the next person at the desk.*
> **Ben:** Hi, Librarian.
> **Me:** Hi, Ben!
> **Ben:** What's your name?
> **Me:** My name's Nicole.
> **Ben:** Hi, Nicole.

And so on. Sometimes he'd chat for a bit longer, but by the time the group was ready to leave, we'd all be "Librarian" again.

One of Ben's favorite topics of conversation was *Naruto*. Ben *loved* the manga series *Naruto*. He always wore the silver etched headband and a blue jacket, doing his best to look like the eponymous character. When I knew Ben would be coming, I would hold on to new copies of the series in anticipation of his visit, since I was the YA librarian at the time and manga and graphic novels fell into my jurisdiction. More often than not, Ben would already be familiar with the copies I had on hand, and he wouldn't hesitate to tell me how far behind I was in my collection development. But that's how we learn, right?

> **Me:** Hi, Ben! Look, I've got number 47.
> **Ben:** [*looks at the book cover*] Do you have *Naruto*, volume 52?
> **Me:** Ummmm . . . [*looking in catalog*]. Shucks, we don't own that one yet.
> **Ben:** Oh, I need volume 52. I already read [*ticks off fingers*] 47, 48, 49, 50, and 51. I need 52.
> **Me:** Oh, I'm sorry. I'll try to have it next time.
> **Ben:** Okay. Be sure you have it next time.
> **Me:** Okay, I'll try.

Ben was also a bit of a movie buff. The group he was part of could only check out books, not DVDs, so, if time allowed, once he had finished working his way through the stacks, he would take his time looking at the DVD cases we had out for patrons to peruse. The arrangement of the circulation and reference desks meant I couldn't quite see the entire children's area, but from my limited viewpoint at the reference desk, I would see Ben carefully take a DVD case off the shelf, read the cover, and put it back.

One day, as the group was taking their leave, Ben came over to say his usual goodbye. *These* exchanges might go something like this:

> **Ben:** Bye, Librarian. Will you have *Naruto*, volume 52, next time?
>
> **Me:** I'll try to have it, Ben. Did you find anything good today?
>
> **Ben:** Yeah. I found some good things. I'll get volume 52 next time. I love coming to the library. See ya later.
>
> **Me:** We love it when you visit us, Ben. Have a great day!

And off he'd go to wait with his group for the HandiVan. On this particular day, though, Ben said something about an activity we had set up. "I love coming to the library," he said. "There are fun activities here." I didn't want to keep him, so I smiled and said thank you, but I was puzzled: because of the short time the group usually stayed, we didn't plan any hands-on activities for their visit. What did Ben mean by "activities"?

I wandered over to our YA manga collection, where I knew Ben usually started his visit. Nothing was out of the ordinary there. My new books display didn't include any games either. Sometimes I left Library Bingo sheets lying around for kids to fill out, with boxes like "Name the title of a book with a blue cover" or "Who wrote *White Fang*?"; if a kid got five in a row, he could come up to the desk and claim a prize. But I hadn't run off any new Bingo sheets. Maybe Ben just equated the whole library visit with an activity?

I then happened to check the children's DVD shelves, Ben's other favorite go-to spot. While my collection development responsibilities also included updating our DVD and CD collections, children's movies fell under the umbrella of the children's librarian, and that collection had its own shelving area. I'm not sure what I was expecting to find, but when I noticed the shelves I paused, and upon closer inspection, burst out laughing. *All* of the covers had been taken out of title order and replaced on the shelves in order by color. It was a very pretty sight, actually: a spectrum of hues, from Barbie pink to Bob the Builder blue and everything in between. Approximately 600 DVDs had been arranged like a box of crayons.

This was Ben's activity. And who knows how often he had played this game? I had noticed him over there nearly every time he and his group came to visit. Was he rearranging our DVDs every time he went over there? Take a DVD off the shelf and put it back next to a similar color?

I ran to get our children's librarian to share with her (what I thought was) this super-fun news. Scarlett didn't seem as charmed by Ben's game as I was, though. "How often has Ben played this game?" I asked. Apparently, *every time he came*. Scarlett had known for a while that this was what Ben did with the DVDs. And she had been quietly putting them back in order after every visit.

As I helped Scarlett rearrange the collection, I couldn't help but giggle at the thought that here we were, supposed "experts" in the field of cataloging and organizing, fixing someone else's idea of a properly ordered DVD collection (and at least one of us feeling a little frustrated while doing so). I wondered if Ben felt the same way: "Sheesh! Every time I come here those librarians have these shelved wrong!" I shared this with Scarlett, and we both cracked up (ironically earning us a stern "Shhh!" from one of the patrons). I admired our children's librarian for not getting mad at Ben or ever telling him to stop. Sure, she sighed when she saw what he'd done (again). Yet she saw beyond the hassle of picking up after a kid: Ben was having a good time, and she wanted him to feel welcome in her space.

I still get a chuckle when I think about it, though.

Ben and his group had visited the library many times, but this was the first time I really wondered what they thought when they came for their visits. Did our space make sense to them? Did they find what they were looking for, or were they content to simply browse? Most importantly, did they have a good time? A lot of the group members were lower functioning than Ben, and it wasn't always possible to connect with them all in the short span of their visit. I soon found myself moving on to school librarianship, where I tried to put in place everything I had learned as a public librarian. Getting to work even closer with special needs students, I was grateful for the short time I'd had to spend with Ben and his group, even if it was just to be a friendly face in the library.

Ben's Game, as I have taken to thinking of this episode, certainly was a lesson in perspective: the right way of doing something for one person may be completely different for another. My biggest takeaway from this experience, however, was the idea of "play." I still love the idea that Ben found a game where there wasn't one—or at least not one planned. Working as I do now with students, I constantly try to incorporate our collection into our lessons through scavenger hunts, relays through the stacks, shelf challenges ("Who can arrange these books the fastest?"), and other activities. I figure if the library isn't a fun place, kids aren't going to want to be there, and I don't want my space to ever be a "have-to." I want it to be a "get-to." I really enjoy being at my job, and I try to make sure my students enjoy being there, too.

14

Prudie's Letter

~ VALERIE CARROLL ~

Public librarians and library workers are often on the front lines of defending those who have been left behind by our social support systems. People living in poverty, people who fall through the cracks of our education system, people facing job loss, people affected by discrimination in their communities—these people rely on libraries and their staff when they have nowhere else to go. Working at a service point gives you a unique perspective on the ways our society fails people in need and gives you a unique opportunity to help them.

I am not a librarian. I have a master's degree in English and spent a couple of years teaching freshman composition as an adjunct instructor at my university. My spouse was offered a job in Arkansas, and I moved without any sort of job lined up there. As a result, I spent seven months unemployed and depressed and lonely. I happened to be in Barnes & Noble looking at knitting pattern books when another customer let me know there was a knitting group that met regularly on Thursdays at the local public library. So the next Thursday, I went to the library at noon. It was the first time I'd ever been to that library. I was much younger than the other people who attended the group, and I had very little in common with them except knitting, but I ended up having a blast and becoming a regular. The librarian who led the group was the library's director, and after a few months, she asked me about my background. When I told her about my degree and teaching experience, she asked me to apply for an opening in their Information Services department. I was hired as a clerk, and my main job was to help patrons at the front desk. Although I eventually grew into additional duties, working the front desk was my first introduction to the library and the people it served, and I still consider it the most important thing I did when I was there.

I have been lucky enough in my life to be mostly insulated from the factors that put other Americans at risk. I am white, I am relatively healthy, I grew up in a middle-class rural community, my parents are still together, and school has always been easy for me. Working at the library made me realize my privilege in a very visceral way. Poverty is not kind, and this is especially true in rural Arkansas. Many legislators in our state do not prioritize social safety nets. And when people fall through the cracks, they come to the library.

I went from interacting with educated college students to working with a much broader range of people. I found it shocking at the time how many people live without teeth or dentures, without needed medical interventions, without legal assistance, without running water. And that core value of public library service—help to all without judgment—is sometimes a person's last line of defense before life goes from bad to worse.

The idea that everything, even just the air conditioning, in a public library is free for all to use affects every interaction between the library's staff and its users and allows them to build relationships that are transformative rather than transactional. But the fact that these bonds are so often built precisely because of failing social safety nets and entrenched inequality is an ugly facet of this truth.

It's a difficult feeling to express: being proud of one's work while regretting the fact that it is necessary, and railing against a broken system by picking up a few of its shards. But I do know that when I worked the front desk, I found in myself a deep well of patience and understanding I didn't know I had. And I was always saddened when I wasn't able to help someone, which was more often that I like to think about: the man who used a wheelchair and had been cut from Medicaid, the unemployed older adults who tried so hard to find a new job but couldn't, the homeless people trying to find a place to stay (the Salvation Army in a city with 70,000 residents has *six* beds and is the only general-use shelter in town). I did what I could, trying to find out what services they needed to contact to get help. But so often, these services didn't exist. Or they existed, but the agencies responsible had very little information available, and no person to contact for questions. And if there were guidelines or official processes, they weren't clearly communicated and seemed arbitrary.

It is absolutely necessary for librarians and other library professionals to call our social institutions to account for the poor quality of information and lack of help available, so that these social services are truly accessible. And we must develop good relationships with those government agencies and nonprofits that provide services in order to effectively advocate for our patrons and connect them to available help. Libraries across the nation are developing innovative strategies for approaching these challenges. But this change starts on the front lines, with the people who interact daily with the library's users.

Every person who works at a library has patrons with whom they've built up a special rapport. One of mine was an African American woman named Prudie. She had two teenage sons who often came with her to the library. Most of the time, she just needed help with run-of-the-mill library reference questions, and I helped her find materials and assisted her with computer questions frequently. She was always very friendly and open with me, and over time, she told me a little bit about her life. She had grown up as one of ten children in one of the poorest areas in the state. She was very proud of her boys, but was very worried about them as well—she wanted to give them opportunities she hadn't had while growing up, but life hadn't made that easy for her. Sometimes she had trouble making ends meet, but she loved the fact that the library offered her a safe place to bring her sons for free, all the books they could read and movies they could watch, access to the internet, and free concerts and classes.

One day, Prudie came up to me at the help desk. She was visibly agitated, and I asked her if everything was okay. It wasn't. She had just picked her sons up from school, where an administrator had informed her that they would be placing her youngest boy in an alternative education program for the remainder of his sophomore year. He had a learning disability and had been having a hard time keeping up with assignments.

Prudie was incensed with her son's teacher and the school's administration; she felt like they had failed her son and were now going to kick him out. She was terrified about her son getting involved in drugs or being targeted for violence—and she was sure that this change was going to lead to just that. I had a hard time following parts of her story because she was so angry; I wanted to help Prudie but didn't know what I could do. She said she wanted to go talk to the school, but was afraid of getting tongue-tied or, worse, losing her temper and making an already difficult situation worse.

I knew the story would sound much different coming from the teacher of Prudie's son. And as someone who was raised by public educators and knows how hard they work for their students, I initially felt sure the whole thing must be a misunderstanding. And anyway, if her son wasn't succeeding in his class, wouldn't an alternative education program be better for him? While our region may lag in other social services, the state of Arkansas does a much better job of funding alternative education programs than neighboring Southern states. But I also know that African-American parents and children often have vastly different experiences with the same educational system. African-American students, especially boys, are often seen as troublemakers first and children second, and receive harsher and more frequent discipline than their white peers for the same behaviors. This is especially true in our area, where the number of teachers of color is disproportionately low compared to the makeup of the general population.

While I didn't know if I could help keep Prudie's son in his school, the one thing I knew I could do was help her communicate her concerns.

"I don't know if it will do any good," I said, "and I can't pretend to be an expert on school policies, but I'd like to help you write a letter to the administrator and the teacher. A letter would let you organize what you need to say, and it will give you the chance to communicate the things you are angry about without losing your temper in person."

"I don't think I could—I'm not much of a writer, and I can't type too well," Prudie said.

"You need to make your case," I said, "and you need to do it in the way that is most likely to persuade your son's school. I think my background in teaching writing could be helpful, and I know how important this is to you."

"I'm willing to do anything—just tell me what to do."

I paused. It was a busy day at the front desk, and I thought that having some more time to process the news would help Prudie collect her thoughts. "If you're free tomorrow afternoon, let's get together and work on it—how is 2:00 p.m.?"

The next day, Prudie showed up with a file folder of documentation from the school about her son: report cards, official Individualized Education Program for his learning disability, progress letters. We sat at a round vinyl-topped table with a sea of papers and a library laptop.

I asked her to do an exercise I often did with my writing students. Many of my freshmen felt insecure about communicating in academic language. They would write convoluted sentences that were devoid of meaning in an attempt to sound "smarter" than they felt they really were.

"Stop worrying about how you sound," I told Prudie. "We're going to ignore the keyboard right now—just tell me what you want to say. Tell me your side of the story and what you want to happen next and why. It's important for you to hear your ideas out loud."

So she told me about her son: about his late diagnosis of dyslexia and attention deficit disorder, about how he struggled so hard with homework and paying attention in class, how the school had promised help and resources that never materialized. She told me about the young men in their neighborhood who targeted teenage boys as potential customers for the drugs and guns they sold, and how she was afraid to leave her sons at home alone even though they were teenagers. She told me it was better for her sons, and for her peace of mind, for them to be at the same school where they could look after each other and walk home together.

As Prudie spoke, I took notes. When she was done, I showed her how to construct a thesis statement in order to distill her argument down and provide the structure for presenting her argument; and together, we wrote an outline to match. And then we slowly worked on writing the letter itself. I talked to her about knowing her audience, the values educators tend to have, and the kind of evidence they would find compelling. It took over an hour, between Prudie's typing and my wording suggestions, to write the letter. But in the end, we had a three-quarter-page letter advocating for her son and asking that the school provide an accessible learning environment in his current classroom.

A few weeks later, Prudie came back to the library. It was the first time I had seen her in a while, and I had been hoping for an update. She walked in the door with her two sons behind her and smiled widely when she saw me.

"I have to tell you," she said, "it worked! They let him stay!"

"That's great to hear," I said, smiling back.

"Thank you," her youngest son said shyly.

"I'm glad I could help," I said, "but your mom is really the one fighting for you. I just helped with the words."

Prudie gave me a hug. After her boys wandered away to browse the DVDs, she told me a bit more. Her letter had convinced the administration to try an option that would keep her son at the same school and in the classroom, but with more one-on-one assistance. As a result, he was doing much better in classes. I was so proud of Prudie for the confidence she'd gained in her ability to advocate for him.

Prudie continued to visit the library during my tenure there, and later on she showed me pictures of both her sons at their high school graduations. I continued to help her when she visited the library; even when I moved to a position that took me away from my work at the front desk, she would often ask for me, just to say hello.

When I eventually decided to leave the library, the thought of leaving Prudie and all the other people I'd come to know there made that choice much harder than expected. Though my current work allows me to help libraries across the nation, I will always miss that feeling of being able to help someone with something they need in the very personal way that working at a library service point affords.

I am exceedingly grateful to have worked in such a wonderful place as my library. Our leadership put customer service first and called on everyone to use their expertise to help others to make the library, and our community, a better place. And for a writer and technical communicator like myself, being able to help Prudie with her letter was a truly memorable way for me to do so. Words have their own power, even when wielded by those who have the least, and being able to demonstrate this to someone in such a concrete way is a writing teacher's dream. And being able to marshal my education and skills to help someone else help herself is a library professional's dream. No matter what your expertise—computers or comics, history or handicrafts, mysteries or mushrooms—working at the front desk of the public library will ensure you can use your skills to make a positive impact in your community.

Simple Positive Play

~ JENNIFER ILARDI ~

n late July 2014, I decided to design my own children's library. I had just started graduate school for my master's degree in library and information science. It was during one of the mandatory residency sessions when an icebreaker included the question, "If you won the lottery, what would you do with the money?" that led me to think more creatively about my goals. I had always wanted to develop some sort of fun learning space for my hometown in Missouri, but it was a far-fetched dream because how many people actually win the lottery?

Throughout that residency week, there were many discussions about being a facilitator and not a dictator, or, as my professor would state, "A guide on the side and not a sage on the stage." I had many opportunities to consider how a library looks and impacts different communities. Before I left my residency, I decided that I was going to start an activity and see if it could be supported by the community.

On August 9, 2014, Michael Brown was killed by a police officer in Ferguson, Missouri. The outrage this incident generated was very palpable, and it created a nationwide conversation that lasted for months.

The voices of those who wanted to change things in the community were overwhelming. I watched a frustrated community on TV. A community that I worked in but didn't live in was hurting. All I wanted to do was make it better. I had a lot of anger, compassion, and confusion in my heart, and my idea of a solution was to bring popsicles and spaghetti. I didn't do it. My husband was working nights, and I had my six-year-old to think about. Some might question my courage and dedication for not demonstrating in the street, but the protests energized my efforts to add positivity to communities through free resources.

I nervously asked my parents if I could host an event in their driveway that would provide kids with access to playful resources. My parents were more than willing to lend me their space, and I hosted my first event in late August 2014. I called it Simple Positive Play.

Simple Positive Play

In the beginning, Simple Positive Play was mainly an experiment for me to see what kind of support I could get for a playful resource library. I knew that I wasn't going to charge for these events, and it took a lot of convincing for me to even request donations. If I hosted a few open play sessions and no one came, then I probably would have set the project aside to revisit it later. However, as I started to talk about my project, I realized it was a concept that could easily be replicated in other communities.

I went from hosting an open play program in the driveway of my childhood home to borrowing space from a local artist who had some room in the back of her studio. This space provided a more comfortable indoor environment with more tables and chairs, and slightly better parking. Eventually, I started open play sessions at the local YMCA.

There were several people who asked whether I wanted Simple Positive Play to be a nonprofit or a for-profit organization. This was something that I hadn't considered initially. I thought that I could just provide stories, books, and activities wherever I went. It took the Ferguson City Council and a special donor to help push me to a different level.

In 2015, a parent who was aware of my efforts informed me about a city building in Ferguson that was no longer being used. The building was full of extra cubicle parts, counters, and lighthouses (apparently a former city official was very fond of these). I was presented with the opportunity to share my idea with the city council and mayor, and ask for use of the vacant building. It was not the easiest presentation to deliver. I was very intimidated. The city of Ferguson was under great scrutiny at the time, so communicating that the goal of Simple Positive Play was to add value was extremely important.

The demands of the city council included adding more legitimacy to Simple Positive Play by getting adequate insurance and obtaining a 501(c)(3) non-profit status. Another requirement was to define our target age group because there were other organizations providing frequent activities for students. The goal for the space in Ferguson was to provide activities for children from birth to the third grade, and I successfully filed for our nonprofit status and obtained proper insurance.

The next step was to work closely with the Parks and Recreation Department. They agreed to clean out the building, paint the walls, and deep-clean the carpets. Because the building had previously been the Parks and Recreation office, there was a lot of wear and tear to the carpet. An interested community member wanted to take a look at the space and watch the progress of this project to bring free play activities to Ferguson. Upon seeing the old carpet, she concluded that it wasn't the best carpet for young children to crawl and walk on. She asked me to obtain a quote to get the carpet replaced. I provided a quote of $4,000 to replace the carpet in the building, and she returned with a check for $10,000 to both replace the carpet and purchase valuable resources for the space.

On July 17, 2016, the more permanent space for Simple Positive Play opened for business. We welcomed seven families and a total of ten children. Since then, we've welcomed hundreds of children. We are mainly open Sundays because that is one of the only days that I am consistently off work from my job at the library. Due to the demand, we enlisted the help of volunteers to make the space available for at least one evening and one weekday morning each month. The space includes resources for gross and fine motor play as well as costumes, trains, books, games, puzzles, and more.

A Family-Friendly Environment

Many different families use our space for their children. Working parents and stay-at-home moms and dads looking for a change in their children's play environment attend. Sometimes grandparents, aunts, or uncles bring kids to engage in the space. And some parent groups have decided that Simple Positive Play is the best place to meet. Some families live close by, while others live twenty minutes or more away, but they make the trek to the space because it is free and welcoming. The fact that there is a lake and an outdoor playground at the park next to our location helps, too.

Our space isn't particularly large, so it's easy to observe interactions between adults and children and also between the children of families from different backgrounds. One heartwarming characteristic I've witnessed is the interaction of people from different religions. Of course, it isn't a requirement for families to disclose their beliefs, but some families explain that the reason they can't attend on certain days is because of religious-based obligations. Some of the women wear hijabs, and one mother feels comfortable enough in the space to take it off if no males are present. Some families simply share the practices that help them feel balanced from day to day. I don't know everyone's personal beliefs, but the value of creating an environment where families feel safe to share and play is not lost on me.

Damian

I know I'm not supposed to have one favorite kid to work with, which is why I have several dozen. But one kid that I'm always delighted to see is Damian. He has platinum blond hair and a smile that makes me want to give him every toy, candy, and flavor of ice cream all at once. He's two. Most of the time, he's very social with me and is interested in where the music is coming from on my computer. On some days, though, he won't leave his mother's side. He's my buddy and I definitely have my moods from time to time, so I don't take it personally.

Both of Damian's parents are recovering addicts. His parents were trying to get clean even before they realized they were about to bring him into the world. I've spoken to the mother quite a bit, and she shares her experiences and her desire to help others who are currently going through a difficult time. There were times, before Damian, when they were homeless. It is possible that her struggle to not use is an obstacle that has haunted her. However, the mom's diligence with regard to her son's well-being is genuine.

Damian's parents have been dedicated to providing a positive environment for him. One of my favorite things about Simple Positive Play is that no matter who you are, what you do, or what you believe, you're welcome. I have never had an incident where a caregiver actively kept one kid from playing with another.

Super Full-Time Librarian

Between working at a public library and starting an organization that promotes free resources, I consider myself a "super full-time" librarian. The job doesn't end because I walk out of a building. I've been approached through my personal social media page about reader's advisory. There has been a time or two when I've been at the public zoo or the grocery store and parents have approached me about upcoming library programs. I was recently pulled out of line at the airport by a TSA agent and another agent commented, "My grandkids love you." These kinds of connections to people and resources have the potential to extend across the country and the world.

Overall . . .

My work in libraries has helped me realize that ideas are just the beginning of a journey. I get the opportunity to listen, learn, and connect using available resources. Libraries can look so different in different communities, but librarians don't need a building to be relevant.

I'm sure that we impact people's lives more than we know. A simple transaction of successfully checking out materials could be the one thing that goes as expected in a person's day. Providing an environment for playful interactions and engaging with other parents makes a difference, and I'm thrilled to do it.

I still work as a youth librarian at a local public library and feel privileged to work in communities that support learning, togetherness, and information.

16

Validation Enough for Me

~ N A N C Y   H O W E ~

n the early 1990s, I graduated as a new librarian and was excited to begin my second career, after being a chemist for many years. And in 2012 I began my career as a public librarian. What had made me initially change careers after years as a chemist? And how did I end up in a public library after almost twenty years as both a corporate and systems librarian? Here's my story . . . read on, it ends better than I could ever have imagined.

For ten years, I worked as an environmental chemist. It took me less than three years after getting a degree in chemistry to realize that I had made a huge mistake. In laboratories with a handful of colleagues, I still felt alone, isolated, and wondering if anything I was doing really mattered.

Long talks with my husband, coupled with his recent appointment to a position at Syracuse University, led to my taking two classes with Dr. Deidre Stam at Syracuse's School of Information Studies. Her enthusiasm for the library profession inspired me to want to matriculate into the program. I was going to be a librarian!

Most of the friends I made in those first few classes graduated long before me. I could not afford to stop working and go to school full-time, so I remained a chemist while taking one class each semester. Going at a slow pace and having a baby in the middle of graduate school meant it took me seven years to do what most people were doing in two years or less. But I did it.

Less than one month after leaving Syracuse, I landed my "dream job"—a corporate librarian for an engineering firm. I was going to be able to manage my own library while still using my background in the sciences. How lucky could I be?

But after six years of working with many talented engineers and scientists and using those undergraduate skills I didn't want to waste, something still wasn't right. I was the only librarian in an organization of over 400 people, which meant I had no one to consult with when I ran into a research dilemma, and no one to discuss new ideas with after attending a conference. My bosses and colleagues were very supportive when I came back from a Special Libraries Association conference ready to replace our library's print resources with CDs—we were even going to get external CD players for free! And everyone was intrigued when I insisted that we had to invest in this new technology—the internet. It was even agreed that the first computer with internet access should be in the library so I could assist with searching. But despite their support, I was still feeling alone. I needed to be with my own kind.

In 1998, I began working for the Central New York Library Resources Council, one of nine such systems in New York state. Finally, I was working with other people who spoke my language. I provided professional services such as continuing education opportunities and technical services for all types of librarians in a four-county region. I was often on the road visiting libraries, seeing where and how others worked. I learned a great deal about my chosen profession and made many friends. I was beginning to feel like a "real librarian."

Over the next twelve years, I worked with many wonderful people on a wide variety of activities. With a group of other librarians, I promoted state-funded online resources to businesses at chamber of commerce trade shows. I taught classes throughout our region, demonstrating how virtual worlds could be used in classroom education. I even filled in as a cataloger for a local school system while the librarian in charge of technical services was on maternity leave. Everywhere I went, I knew that people appreciated and valued the work I was doing.

One day I was talking with one of the public library directors in our region. Half-jokingly, I asked if I could come to her library for a day to see what being a "real librarian" was like. She took me up on this offer, as the holidays were approaching and she would be short-staffed. With my boss's blessing, I spent a day between Christmas and New Year's working at Syracuse's Beauchamp Library, a branch of the Onondaga County Public Library System.

I spent my day doing a bit of everything: I checked out materials at circulation (and broke a Dynix wand in the process). I pulled the "holds" so materials could be sent to other libraries in the system. And I spent part of the afternoon helping with a Kwanzaa program after working the reference desk for an hour. I talked to patrons of all ages as the eight hours flew by. At the end of the day, I was a "real librarian," and I was hooked. I had found the place I wanted to be. But how would I get there?

It took a few more years, but eventually the opportunity presented itself. The Baldwinsville Public Library (in Onondaga County) was looking for a reference librarian who could also run a two-year, state-funded grant program. The director asked me if I was interested because I had administered many of these programs and could hit the ground running. I welcomed the change. Little did I know how much I myself would change as a result of this new job.

Running any grant-funded project requires forms and reports; I could do that easily given my previous experience. What I had little experience in was working with the general public. I had always worked with specific groups of people—engineers, scientists, librarians. Except for those eight hours at Beauchamp, I was new to the world of the public library.

One of our library's target populations was the unemployed and underemployed. We spread the word that there would be resume assistance offered at the library every day from 9:00 a.m. to 5:00 p.m. during the week. Armed with resume and cover-letter help books and my newly issued laptop, I was ready for my first appointment. Would it be a new college graduate looking for that first job? Would it be a stay-at-home mom ready to reenter the workforce? No, it was a meat processor from the local turkey farm that had just closed its doors. The gentleman had mechanically deboned turkeys for twenty-two years, his only job after finishing high school. He came to the library convinced that he had no marketable skills. We talked at length. What he didn't recognize were the skills and attributes he *did* have. Longevity—twenty-two years at the same company was to be commended. He had done his work well enough to train new employees; he didn't realize he was a trainer. He also had a good working knowledge of the OSHA standards that regulated his workplace. As we talked, I could feel his tension subsiding; he was smiling and laughing. He left with a resume, a list of references, and a more hopeful outlook. And it felt good to see him leave happier than when he arrived. Maybe I could help make a difference.

Some people who come to search for work don't come alone. I had often seen a woman come in with her young son, who would sit as quietly as any eight-year-old boy possibly can. As patient as she would try to be, I could see that having him there was a struggle. So one day I offered to have Jason sit in my office. He could color (I am a mom, I have crayons) and keep me company while I did paperwork. His mother was thrilled. Jason made me a very detailed picture of a castle with a drawbridge, a moat, and a king and some knights. He signed it and I hung it on the wall in front of my desk. He continued to visit me in my office while his mom was on the computer. Sometimes he colored, and when I had the time, we read books. That was 2010. Jason is going to be a senior this year and I still have that picture. He still visits me and has introduced me to some of his friends. A short story he recently submitted in a national essay contest was chosen for inclusion in a book—1,500 high school students entered the contest, and only 100 were chosen. And he is now working on a book of his own, hoping to have it published before graduation. He promised that someday when he wins a Pulitzer, he will give his favorite librarian credit. I cried. I knew in that moment I had made a difference.

Jason and I bonded from that first time in my office, but sometimes you don't realize the effect you have on someone until one day they let their guard down and show you. Keith visits the library daily when he is between jobs, which is more often than I am sure he would like. He comes to escape a mother who makes life difficult. With us, he can play computer games, look at Facebook, and read whatever he likes without judgment. He seemed to prefer the other librarians, never talking to me. He told one of my colleagues that I scare him because I tend to walk around the building at a fast pace and always seem busy. That is true . . . I do walk fast, and usually I am caught up in my own thoughts. But one day while I was working at the reference desk, Keith overheard a patron giving me a hard time. While I don't recall the reason why this gentleman was so angry, I do know that I was trying to calm him down, to no avail. As he stormed off, I noticed Keith walking over to him. He stopped the man, pointed his finger in the man's face and said, "You don't talk to my family like that in my house!" The man quickly left the building and Keith returned to his computer. I was shocked. But I realized that while I might seem less approachable than others, Keith was looking out for me. After that, I made sure that when I saw him, I smiled and said hello. We have had some pleasant conversations, and I don't think he views me as quite so scary now. And knowing that he feels comfortable around me, well, that makes my day!

Some of my favorite library moments have been outside the walls of the building. Up until I began working at Baldwinsville, I didn't have any experience working with senior citizens. I was approached to start a book club at the local senior center across the street from our library. After a discussion with the activities coordinator at the center, we agreed on an audiobook club. I would go once each week and we'd listen to a book together. That way we'd all be "on the same page." And to make it more fun, we'd choose books that were also movies. After reading the book, we'd watch the movie and compare them. Nervous at first, I went over to the senior center with *The King's Speech*. Would they like the book I had picked? Would they like me? As it turned out, they couldn't wait to delve into something more interesting than playing Bingo or making crafts. And they welcomed me like they had known me for years! In the last seven years, we have covered a wide range of topics in our readings, taking turns at choosing the titles.

Of course, in a situation like this you tend to become closer to some people. Jack and I hit it off right from the start. We would always sit near each other. He reminded me of my father, and he had a daughter near my age. We both cried while listening to *Unbroken* and giggled together while watching the film version of *A Walk in the Woods*. Jack was my buddy. He even visited me in the library. His favorite author was James Lee Burke. I found all the large-print books by Burke I could, and he was always so grateful. When the coordinator called to say that Jack had had a stroke and was not expected to make it, I cried. To this day I can't walk into the center without thinking of him. He was my Jack. Because of him and the others I spend Friday mornings with, senior citizens have become my favorite group of people, in and out of the library.

If someone had told me nine years ago that not only would I be participating in story hours, but I would refuse to give up my group when the new children's librarian was hired, I would say they were crazy. But that is exactly what happened. When our previous children's librarian became ill, I grudgingly took on the littlest people, the 6- to 24-month-old babies and their caregivers. I have children and I like their friends, but I don't gush at the sight of babies. Well, now I do . . . at least some of them.

I went in on Tuesday at 9:30 a.m. It was my first storytime. I was armed with two books and one song, and I promised myself that if I got out of there alive, my husband was taking me to dinner, and there would be wine. I sat down in my rocking chair and realized after about thirty seconds that no one under the age of two was paying attention to me. They were more interested in the toys on the floor. The caregivers, mostly women, were listening politely. This was not doing my ego any good, nor did it make me want to return next week. Something had to change.

One week later: armed with two more books and the remote to the big-screen television mounted on the wall, I went in. On went the TV, and a YouTube video of 5 *Little Monkeys Jumping on the Bed* began to play. I sang, I danced, and suddenly, I had their attention! Some were smiling and some were clapping. The attention waned a bit while I read, but that was okay. I had a plan for next week.

On the third Tuesday, we began with a video, went on to two books, and ended with another video. After that, I stayed on the floor and began to play with them. I crawled through the tunnel. I played ball. I pretended to eat plastic pizza. They were starting to notice me. And they wanted to play with me!

A year later, I have several new friends among the kids. Owen looks for me if I'm not there (his grandmother told me he shrugs, holds out his hands, and says, "Where is she?"). And Mila helps me read by sitting on my lap and turning the pages. My heart melts when I get hugs and kisses from Elise and Rory. And the high-fives from Jack are priceless. I told all of them that they are not allowed to grow up and leave Miss Nancy's class. But of course, they are, and new friends are taking their place. When our new librarian started in the fall, I "offered" to keep my Tuesday group. She was grateful for the help, and I didn't have to arm wrestle her for it. Those are my babies and no one else can have them . . . Who would have predicted that?

These stories highlight why I wake up every morning, happy to go to work because I love what I do. When I was eighteen, I wanted to be a scientist. I would be the first woman in my family who wasn't going into a traditional female profession. I come from a long line of teachers, administrative assistants, and yes, even librarians. I was going to validate my self-worth by being different from the others, by being "smarter." I have no idea what I was thinking of back then.

I was professionally miserable until I graduated with my library degree. And even then, it wasn't until I began working in a public library that I saw the difference I could make to someone else. When you suggest a book to an elderly patron who needs something to read over the weekend and they thank you profusely, you've made a difference. When you help someone learn Microsoft Publisher so they can create a family history book for their family reunion, you've made a difference. When you stop by someone's house to see why their printer isn't working and they can't afford to call the Geek Squad, you've made a difference. When a patron loses her spouse and looks for you because you knew him and she needs a shoulder to cry on, you know you've made a difference. And that is validation enough for me.

I Worked a Lifetime to Become Homeless

~ FRANK JACKSON with BEN BIZZLE ~

t was 3:30 on a Sunday afternoon in the winter of 2010. I was sitting on the hard concrete steps of the Salvation Army shelter, waiting for it to open. I was scared, I was humiliated, I was heartbroken, and I was officially homeless. More than anything else, I was trying to wrap my head around what in my life I had done to deserve this.

Growing Up

I was born in the small town of Leachville, Arkansas, on December 28, 1963. My mother and grandmother raised me. I knew who my father was, but I never knew him and he wasn't a part of my life. Growing up, we were poor, but we survived. My mother and grandmother were very strict. They told me what to do, and generally, I did what I was told. They basically made all my decisions for me until I was eighteen years old. I was a good kid.

The most trouble I ever got into growing up was when I was about ten years old. I was over at Maynard's General Store about a mile from our house. They had a box full of one-cent balloons, and I pocketed one of those balloons. Later, when I got home and blew up the balloon, my mother asked me where I got it and I started to cry. She said, "You stole it, didn't you?" Then she had me go outside and pull a willow switch off the tree in the front yard, and she whipped me every step of the way from our house to that store . . . and we took the long way around. She made me go in there, pay for that balloon, and tell them what I'd done. Meanwhile, she was out front cutting a new switch off their tree because she'd worn out the one from the house. She then proceeded to whip me all the way back home. But I learned my lesson. From that day forward, I have never in my life stolen anything else from anybody.

At school, I was a decent student. I hated homework, but I read a lot. If you gave me a book to read, I could remember just about everything in it. That helped me a lot in my studies, particularly in history and English. It also established a deep love of reading at a very young age. Reading was something I was good at and I enjoyed. I wasn't the best student, but I studied hard and made decent grades. In 1982, I graduated from Manila High School with a 3.25 grade point average.

Adulthood

When I graduated from high school, I didn't really know what I wanted to do. I went to Vo-Tech school at Cotton Bowl Vo-Tech in Burdett, Arkansas, for a year and a half, where I studied air-conditioning repair, sheet metal fabrication, and things like that. I managed to pick up some skills that served me well over the years.

It was fall when I graduated from Vo-Tech school, and fall is cotton-ginning season in Arkansas. I went up to the Sandusky Gin in Manila, Arkansas, and asked the man for a job, and he gave me one. Little did I know at the time, but that was the beginning of a 26-year career in cotton. From one gin being bought out by another, and then another, I continued to work in the industry. Over the years, I worked for some really good people. I was a press operator, which meant I was responsible for running the machine that bailed the cotton. I was told often that I was good at it, and a number of farmers said they used our gin because of the work I did.

I started out working part-time, seasonally, making $3.35 an hour. By the time my career was over, I was working full-time for a huge ginning operation, making $10.50 an hour, with benefits. While I wasn't rich, I always made enough money to make ends meet. Living is pretty cheap in rural Arkansas.

The early years were probably the most memorable ones. That first gin ran off twin diesel engines that were the same engines used in World War II PT boats. They were old, cantankerous engines that you had to baby all the time to keep running. They ran so hot that we had one old guy who used to use them to cook for us. He'd fry bacon and eggs on the manifolds of those old engines. He'd wrap canned biscuits in aluminum foil and cook them, too. The food had a lot of gin dust in it and tasted of diesel fuel sometimes, but on an empty stomach at 3:00 in the morning, when it was about 25 degrees outside, we were too busy eating to waste time complaining.

By 2003, I was working full-time for Cotton Growers, Inc., in Dell, Arkansas, and I began to develop some health problems. Mainly because of the physical demands of my job, I started suffering from arthritis. Also, although it wasn't diagnosed until much later, I had diabetes and had put on a significant amount of weight. You see, in a cotton gin, one of the skills you must have is the ability to climb. There's a lot of climbing into cotton trailers, up ladders, and on equipment. I continued to work as hard as I could through the pain, but there were times when it was too much. As a result of this, coupled with a sharp downturn in the cotton market, I would sometimes be reduced to part-time labor. It was tough for me because I had always been a hard worker, and I wasn't able to do the things I used to do. I felt like I was letting myself down and letting my employer down. But these were good people, and they did their best to accommodate my physical challenges where they could. For the next several years, I continued to work through the pain. Cotton-ginning was all I'd ever done. It was all I really knew how to do.

In September 2010, we were about two weeks into ginning season, and I went to work one morning though I wasn't feeling well. It was hot in the gin and the machines were running all out. We were working at full speed, and at some point, though I don't remember it happening, I was told that I got a blank look on my face and then simply pitched forward, face-down onto the concrete. When I came to, I was in the arms of my gin supervisor and there were people standing around crying. Little old Hispanic ladies were holding their rosary beads, praying, because they thought I had died.

My career in cotton was over. At forty-six years old, I was officially retired from the only thing I knew how to do. And I had no idea what would happen next. The cotton industry is not one where an employee like me has a 401K or stock options, or any of those sorts of things. I didn't have any savings or retirement. The company did give me a little money, but I knew that wouldn't last long. So I moved into the Jamie Bee motel in Jonesboro, Arkansas. It was a ratty little pay-by-the-week place, but I had to try to make my money last as long as I could while I figured out what I was going to do. I wanted to work, but I couldn't find a job. It seemed no one was willing to hire a 46-year-old man with limited skills and a bunch of health issues.

Homeless

In a very short time, my money ran out. I found myself homeless, helpless, and broke. And that brings us back to those steps outside the Salvation Army shelter on that Sunday afternoon. I didn't want to go to the Salvation Army. But I had run through all my options, and it was either that, or I was going to have to sleep beneath an overpass or find a tent and sleep somewhere in that.

When they opened at 4:00 p.m., I went inside and filled out the paperwork. I had no idea what to expect. To me, a homeless shelter was a place full of drunks, dopeheads, and criminals. But then I thought, "Wait, you're homeless, and you aren't any of those things. You're just a sick guy who doesn't have any money." That first day, I was scared to death. I was told that I'd be staying in a dorm with eleven other men, and I thought it was going to be like prison, another place I'd never been but had a lot of ideas of what it must be like.

Over the next few days, I started opening up and talking with the other people living there. I came to realize that people wind up homeless for a lot of different reasons. These were ordinary people, just like me. None of them had ever planned to wind up there, and most of them were looking for a way out. Some of them were characters, to be sure, but none of them were bad people. Some of them were there because they were sick and couldn't work. Some of them had issues, mental or physical, that prevented them from being able to function in a normal living situation, and yes, there were some there as a result of alcoholism or drug addiction. But none of them wanted to be there, and none of them were there because they were just a bunch of lazy bums looking for a free handout. In my experience, that's not what homelessness is. One of the remarkable things about the homeless is their willingness to help one another. There's a certain sense of camaraderie. I witnessed many instances where someone was lucky enough to pick up some day-labor work and would share their money with the other people living at the shelter. The number of times I saw people helping each other far exceeded the number of times I saw people in conflict. While everyone was looking for their own opportunity to get out of the situation, there was a common understanding that for the time being, we were all in this together.

One of the things I don't think people consider when it comes to homelessness is the boredom. People don't really think about how their daily routine occupies so much of their time. Most folks get up in the morning, go to work all day, go home, maybe relax a bit in the evening, go to bed, and do it all over again the next day. It can often feel like there isn't enough time in the day. But when you're homeless, it feels like all you have is time. There is no job to go to for eight hours, or a home to unwind in for a couple hours after a long day, or a bed to sleep in at night and wake up from in the morning. Instead, there is fear and anxiety and self-hate, and lots of time to live in those feelings.

Granted, there were some things to do, things that were required if you wanted to stay at the Salvation Army. One of those requirements was that you had to make an effort to find employment. But that, the thing most of us wanted more than anything else, can be one of the most humiliating aspects of homelessness. On any job application, you're required to provide an address, and for those of us at the shelter, that address was the Salvation Army. However, many employers recognize that address, and it means you're immediately disqualified from consideration for employment. I experienced this firsthand. At one point, I went into a place of business and asked to fill out a job application. I filled it out and turned it in. As I was leaving, I happened to turn around, and I saw the person I'd handed the application to throwing it in the garbage. I went outside, sat down on the curb, and broke down in tears. I was forty-six years old, I was homeless, and after spending my entire life working as hard as I could, these people wouldn't even give me a chance to flip burgers. They wouldn't even talk to me because of my address.

For me, that was the hardest part of being homeless, the dehumanizing effect it has on you. People won't look you in the eye. They won't speak to you. You're treated as though you aren't worthy of acknowledgment. Law enforcement harasses you. On one occasion, I was walking back to the Salvation Army after looking for work, and I cut across a parking lot. A police officer pulled into the lot and asked me what I was doing, and I told him. He then asked me if I knew I was trespassing and told me I needed to stay off private property, that people didn't want my kind around . . . my kind.

The Library

When staying at the Salvation Army shelter, you have to be out every morning before 8:00 a.m., so I learned almost immediately that what many people there did every day was go to the public library. Being an avid reader and having spent quite a bit of time in the library during more successful periods in my life, I found this comforting to learn. Being a history buff, I'd already read almost the entire collection of military history books the library had to offer, all the way from the Civil War through Vietnam. But being homeless and going to the library was different. Previously, I'd go in, look through the books for as long as I wanted, pick the ones I wanted to read, check them out, and leave. I'd probably never spent more than an hour in the library at one time, just long enough to pick out what I wanted and go . . . home. But as a homeless person, it was like I suddenly didn't know how to use the library. Would they really let us all sit around for six or eight hours doing nothing? It seemed like homeless people got run off from anywhere they tried to go. How long would they let you stay at the library until they asked you to leave? I had no idea.

To my surprise, the staff at the library treated me the same as they'd treated me any other time I'd been there. In time, they realized that I was coming in with other people they recognized from the shelter, but that didn't seem to change their attitude toward me. I noticed that they seemed to treat the homeless just like they treated everyone else. They never told anyone they couldn't have another cup of the free coffee, or they couldn't sit in that chair anymore, or they had to get off the public computers. If anything, it seemed like they went out of their way to help us. One day, I was talking with Nathan, one of the guys who worked there, and I mentioned that I was a fan of 1980s "hair bands," specifically Van Halen, and Eddie Van Halen's guitar playing. He got excited and asked if I liked Steve Vai, and what I thought about Joe Satriani. Next, we were sitting at one of the computers and he was pulling up YouTube videos for me to watch. He told me to hang on and ran to get me a pair of free earbuds. As he was coming back, I realized that at that moment, I didn't feel homeless. I didn't feel like he was just being nice to a homeless guy. I felt like a guy talking to another guy about the music they liked. I felt normal.

I did spend quite a bit of time on the public computers. A lot of us from the shelter did. For one thing, having the library's computers available to us made it easier to apply for jobs. But in reality, that doesn't take very long, and after a while, you've pretty much applied to every place you can. Folks at the shelter kept talking about this game on Facebook called Farmville. Long into the night, they'd be talking about their "farms." I thought this was ridiculous at first, but one day I decided to give it a try. And oh my God, was I addicted. You know you're addicted to a video game when you wake up at 3:00 in the morning and realize you'd forgotten to pick your virtual raspberries the day before and have trouble getting back to sleep because you're so frustrated with yourself over it. Looking back now, I laugh at myself, but I also realize it was a real lifeline at the time. The reason the guys at the shelter fretted over their farms so much was that, while we were homeless and basically had nothing in the "real world," there was a sense of ownership in those farms. My farm was mine. I had made some friends online, and their farms were theirs. And together we were a community. No one knew I was homeless. The Frank they knew was a great neighbor managing a successful farm and always willing to lend a hand. I even got a speaking role in one of the library's YouTube videos. To this day, you can go online and watch me stand up in my farmer's cap and overalls and ask, "Does anybody have two nails and a board for my farm in Farmville?"

At least for me, there was no one who reflected the love and compassion of the library more than a lady named Melanie who worked at the front desk. I can't remember a single morning I walked into that library and she was working the desk that she didn't look up with a big smile and say, "Hey, Frank." It wasn't just me. She did this with all of us. She'll never know how much it meant for her to call us by name, to say "hey" to us, to ask how we were doing. Her smile and sincerity let you know that this was a person who genuinely cared about you. One day, I wasn't feeling well at all. I'd broken a wisdom tooth and it was horribly abscessed and infected. Being stubborn and broke, I was just trying to suffer through it. It wasn't getting any better, though. My face was terribly swollen, and I could tell I was running a pretty high fever. I'd only been on the public computer for a few minutes when Melanie came walking over to find out what was wrong, so I explained the situation to her. She put her hand on my forehead, and then she laid into me, "Frank, you're burning up. What do you think you're doing? You've got to go to the emergency room." I tried to protest, but she was having none of it. "If you don't get up right now and go to the emergency room, I'm calling an ambulance. The emergency room has to treat you, and I'm not about to let you die on me." She was obviously not going to take "no" for an answer, so I did what I was told. The folks at the emergency room filled me full of antibiotics and told me how bad the infection was. They explained that if I'd waited a couple more days, chances are it could have killed me. Melanie was the reason I went, the only reason. She cared enough about me to insist, regardless of my place in life, regardless of everything that made my world seem so dark, that I take care of myself. My well-being mattered to her. I mattered to her, personally. She wasn't just doing a job. She was taking care of the people who came into that library. She was looking after us, all of us. As far as I'm concerned, she saved my life that day.

The library is a sanctuary. It gives people a place to be and things to do. There are always programs for us to attend, computers for us to use, music for us to listen to, movies for us to watch, and of course, books for us to read. But it's more than that. I'm not sure if the people at the library are even aware of the level of public service they're providing. For the homeless, being able to go to the library kept us from being harassed or humiliated on the streets. It gives people with alcohol and drug problems a chance to stay sober. It helps keep people out of trouble. There's somewhere you can go where you'll be treated with dignity and respect. The library is staffed by people who care without it seeming like pity. The library gives people a safe place in which to make a positive choice in their life each day.

Brighter Days Ahead

I was homeless for just over ten months. A position became available at the Salvation Army shelter where I'd been staying, and I was fortunate enough to be hired. For a period of time, things didn't really change much, as I was the nighttime supervisor, which basically meant I spent the night at the shelter and made sure everyone followed the rules. But I had a job and was able to save money. I could see myself getting back on my feet. In time, I was able to get a small apartment and continue the process of rebuilding my life. Today, I live in a house by a lake, and I enjoy spending relaxing evenings fishing off the dock out back. A few years ago, I got a job working with mentally challenged men. There are three gentlemen living together in a house, and I go over there every morning. I help them cook, clean, and take care of themselves. Given their challenges, we do a lot of the same things over and over again. Tying shoes and brushing teeth are things they may forget how to do on their own from one day to the next. But I never lose my patience. I never get frustrated with them. I think back to my local library and what I learned from the people who worked there. I treat these men with dignity and respect. I make sure they know that I care about them and their well-being. I share with them all the love I have inside me, one human being to another, just like the people at the library shared with me not so many years ago.

I have no doubt that if it weren't for the Salvation Army and the Jonesboro Public Library, you wouldn't be reading this story. I'd be dead. The Salvation Army gave me a place to sleep and food to eat, and the library gave me a place where I could go and feel human. The library not only allowed me to maintain my dignity; the people there reinforced it. They reminded me of my own value as a human being. You folks have a saying that libraries save lives. I tell this story knowing that mine is one of those lives you saved.

ABOUT THE EDITORS AND CONTRIBUTORS

BEN BIZZLE is the founder and CEO of Library Market, a marketing and web development firm. He is a 2013 *Library Journal* Mover & Shaker, a John Cotton Dana Award winner, and the author of the book *Start a Revolution: Stop Acting Like a Library*. For over seven years, he was the director of technology and head of the creative team at the Craighead County Jonesboro Public Library in Jonesboro, Arkansas.

SUE CONSIDINE is an independent international consultant and the former executive director of the Fayetteville Free Library (FFL) in upstate New York. During her administration, the FFL became a leader of innovation in the library field; it pioneered new transformative methods of community engagement, including the integration of participatory STEAM learning into all library services and the launch of the first ever fabrication lab/makerspace, the FFL FabLab, in a public library. Sue is an experienced public speaker who presents on contemporary library issues such as innovation, leadership, and change management. She is a recipient of the *Library Journal* Mover & Shaker, WCNY Women Who Make America, PLA Charlie Robinson, and the White House "Champion of Change" awards. She has also served in diverse leadership roles in ALA and the International Federation of Library Associations.

Rebekkah Smith Aldrich is the executive director of the Mid-Hudson Library System in New York state. Named a *Library Journal* Mover & Shaker, she is a frequent international speaker on smart, practical ways to ensure the future of our libraries. She is also the author of *Sustainable Thinking: Ensuring Your Library's Future in an Uncertain World* and of *Resilience* (Library Futures Series). Rebekkah is a founding board member of ALA's Sustainability

Roundtable and cofounder of the New York Library Association's Sustainability Initiative, and she serves on the advisory board for ALA's Center for the Future of Libraries.

Tom Bruno began his obsession with libraries as a kid when he would plan his entire week around the arrival of the county library's bookmobile. Since then he has worked in both academic and public libraries, and he also consults on a wide variety of library topics, including collections, resource-sharing, and makerspaces. Tom is the author of two nonfiction books—*Wearable Technology: Smart Watches to Google Glass for Libraries* and *Gaming Programs for All Ages at the Libraries: A Practical Guide for Librarians*—and he self-publishes an anthology of library-themed science fiction titled *L Is for Librarian*. He is also a senior staff writer and editor for EveryLibrary. Tom lives in Connecticut with his wife (also a librarian) and their two children, who pretty much grew up in the library stacks.

Valerie Carroll has an MA in English from Texas Tech University and worked for six years at the Craighead County Jonesboro Public Library in Jonesboro, Arkansas, where she first met Ben Bizzle. In 2017, she left the library to become the chief operating officer of Library Market, the website and software development company that Ben started. She lives in Jonesboro with her family, two housecats, and a mildly embarrassing yarn collection.

Yago Cura is a bilingual outreach librarian with the Los Angeles Public Library and president of the Los Angeles chapter of REFORMA. He also runs HINCHAS Press, which publishes the Librarians with Spines series with the help of Max Macias and Autumn Anglin. He contributed a chapter to Stacy Russo's book *A Better World Starts Here: Activists and Their Work* (2019), and he wrote about the digital divide in South Central Los Angeles in the compendium *Poet-Librarians in the Library of Babel: Innovative Meditations on Librarianship* (2018).

Fayetteville Free Library Team, the staff of the Fayetteville Free Library (FFL) in upstate New York, is an internationally recognized leader of library innovation and strategic change. The FFL serves with intention and purpose, elevating and enhancing the experience of members of the community and contributing in meaningful and substantial ways to the library profession. The FFL is home to the first fabrication lab/makerspace in a public library, the FFL FabLab.

Erica Freudenberger is a collaborator who works with libraries to empower their communities. She is currently the outreach and engagement consultant at the Southern Adirondack Library System, and she formerly led the Red Hook Public Library, which was a finalist for the Best Small Library Award and garnered a five-star rating from 2013 to 2016. Erica contributed to the Aspen Institute's Re-Envisioning Public Libraries pilot, and in 2016 she was named a Mover & Shaker by *Library Journal*. She secured PLA's Library Innovation Award for the Southern Adirondack Library System's Fresh Food Collective Farm-to-Library Distribution in 2019.

Christopher Gallegos was born in Colorado, spent his early childhood in New Mexico, and came of age in rural California. After a stint in a heavy metal band and dabbling with a journalism career, he started working for the Monterey County Free Libraries in 2005. He remains there to this day. As a librarian, his interests include local history, collection development, different weeding methods, and doing silly voices at storytime. Outside of libraries, he enjoys kettlebells, calisthenics, aromatherapy, herbal medicine, Brazilian culture, reggae music, playing acoustic guitar, martial arts and classic horror films, hiking, nature photography, scripture, and praying the rosary.

Nicole Goff loves books, cats, and coffee. She grew up on a steady diet of picture books (thanks, Mom!), pancakes (thanks, Dad!), and make-believe (thanks, siblings!). Needless to say, when she fell into librarianship, it fit as snugly as a well-worn cardigan. Nicole lives with her husband, who is also a librarian, and two furry, wingless dragons, who disguise themselves as cats.

Nancy Howe is the assistant director for the Baldwinsville Public Library in upstate New York. She works cooperatively with many local organizations to bring various programs and services into the community. After earning her MLS degree from Syracuse University, she was employed as the corporate librarian at C&S Companies, and then was the assistant director of the Central New York Library Resources Council.

Jennifer Ilardi is from a small town in northeastern Missouri called Louisiana. She currently lives in St. Charles, Missouri, with her husband, daughter, cat, and her daughter's two birds named Pika and Belle. Her daughter frequently challenges her to create oddly specific costumes, cakes, and invitations. This means Jennifer gets to collaborate with a high-demand client on a regular basis. Jennifer is a huge fan of creating experiences where she can support the design process between and among parents and children. Organizing the resources to make this possible is a welcome challenge for her. She is truly passionate about providing tools for exploration because she has witnessed it leading to community connections in a space where it is permissible to experiment freely.

Frank Jackson spent twenty-six years in the cotton-ginning industry before health problems forced him into homelessness. It was the kindness of the local library and its staff that introduced him to a new skill set, compassionate service. Frank has spent the last ten years giving back to his community, working first with the homeless at the Salvation Army and now with the intellectually disabled. It is a career he loves. He also finds time for his favorite hobby, catching big catfish as often as he can.

Meredith Levine fell in love with libraries when she started volunteering at the New York Public Library. She went on to earn her MLIS degree from Syracuse University while working at the Fayetteville Free Library (FFL). After graduation, she became the director of family engagement at the FFL, helping to lead youth programming centered around STEAM. Meredith moved to Chattanooga, Tennessee, in 2015 and took a position as head of youth services at the Chattanooga Public Library (CPL), where she helped shape the vision of youth programming for the system, and created city-wide efforts that led to more people coming in through the library's doors. She also oversaw the construction and management of the Studio at the CPL, a state-of-the-art professional recording studio that has created opportunities for creatives and musicians. Meredith also helped expand the 4th-floor makerspace to meet more needs in the community. She left the CPL in 2019 and now lives in Los Angeles, where she is the assistant library administrator for adult and digital services at the LA County Library.

Brandy McNeil is a serial innovator who focuses on community needs through game-changing innovations to build successful digital literacy programs. As an award-winning director of digital literacy education for the New York Public Library, Brandy has played a significant role in paving the way for successful series-based programming, as well as coding workshops in public libraries. She built the highly successful TechConnect Department at the library and has tripled program attendance there, making the NYPL one of the most widely attended digital literacy programs in the United States. Brandy holds an MBA in entrepreneurship, is currently pursuing her doctorate in business, and is a sought-after speaker, panelist, and an international authority on tech education.

Melissa M. Powell has been working in libraries since 1980, starting as a shelver at her local public library. She earned her MLIS degree in 1989 from Northern Illinois University. She has worked in public, academic, special, and school libraries in various public, technical, and administrative roles. In 2006, she created her own company working as a consultant for libraries, and in 2017, she started working for a library vendor. Melissa currently lives in Massachusetts with her husband and two cats and competes in Scottish Highland Games for fun. She is also the editor of *Becoming an Independent Information Professional* (2017).

Nicolette Warisse Sosulski was our dear friend. She was the person who would send us Facebook messages, one line at a time, in rapid succession, because she was used to doing that to keep patrons engaged while providing live online reference assistance. She was the person who bought scarves for her friends because she'd see a scarf that reminded her of you. And she was a librarian's librarian. For anyone who knew her, you knew that if you couldn't find it, ask Nicolette because she'd go to the ends of the earth to get you the information you were looking for. In short, she was the best of us.

John Spears started off as a music major at the University of Illinois, briefly switched to social work, and eventually graduated with a degree in musicology. Despite the lucrative possibilities this presented, he went for an MSLIS degree and is now the chief librarian at the Pikes Peak Library District. He lives in Colorado Springs with his partner Brian and two dogs.